Contents

Acknowledgements

A comprehensive book on vocal technique is inevitably a synthesis of work from a number of sources, and there are a few colleagues whom I would like to mention especially. These are: Jo Estill, who helped so many of us back in the 1990s to understand what it was that musical theatre singers were doing; Janice Chapman for her work on 'Primal Connection', Meribeth Dayme (formerly Bunch) for her insight and wisdom into the writing process and for sound practical advice on muscle behaviour; Jacob Lieberman for his valuable insights on laryngeal orienteering, and Richard Lipton for enthusing me about phonetics and for help in developing the concept of 'medialising'.

To my husband, business and teaching partner Jeremy Fisher, I owe huge thanks for helping me face off the demons in writing my first book back in 1998 and for his detailed practical feedback and constructive criticism. Ana Sanderson has proved once again to be an insightful, supportive editor, and I feel fortunate to be working with her.

In addition I must thank colleagues who contributed by reading chapters and taking the time to talk through their observations with me: Tom and Sara Harris, John Rubin, Chris Kell, Meribeth Dayme and, more lately, Matthew Reeve. Elizabeth Stirling made the photographs of models Melody Bridges and Scott Braid – my thanks to all.

Finally I would like to acknowledge those with whom I have worked, both students and co-tutors. You are too numerous to mention, but the shared experience of working with you has helped to develop and shape my understanding thus far.

The author and publishers would like to thank the following who gave permission for the inclusion of copyright material.

Foreword

In preparing the text for *Singing and The Actor*, my aim has been to speak directly to the reader, addressing his or her problems. My prime concerns are about knowledge, ability, security and, ultimately, the health of the vocal performer. This book can be used as a training manual for students of singing and as a resource for teachers and vocal coaches. Information in the book is on three levels: conceptual (the physical and acoustic properties of the instrument), practical (developing awareness and skill, troubleshooting), and aesthetic (applying the work in a specific field). The key principles of technique set out are based on the physical and acoustic properties of the voice. In this sense this book can be used by anyone wanting to discover the 'how' and 'why' of their voice. In terms of practical application and those areas where there are choices to be made, the information is geared towards the practice of Musical Theatre.

Musical Theatre is a relatively recent art form, not even a hundred years old. Its pedagogy is still in its teens. The stylistic and vocal needs of the theatre singer are evolving differently from those of the classical singer, and there is a need for an approach that is specific to the genre. The information in this book is a synthesis of my own practical experience of working for over 20 years in the field, and the work of some respected colleagues. In this second edition I have been able to include new insights into some of the original topics. These include strategies for processing information and developing muscle memory. Those who find it difficult to absorb practical information in written form will find these useful. In addition, there is more detailed information on dealing with range, registers and gear changes. The other major additions are the advancing and mixing of voice qualities, and more reference to the actor's process of decision making. Workshopping the material with numerous actors and teachers has been enormously helpful in shaping these developments.

A colleague has kindly described *Singing and the Actor* as 'a grown-up book'. This means that the text encourages you to take charge of your own voice: to feel, to visualise and to listen for yourself, rather than relying on the teacher to do it for you. The teacher can only provide an environment for change by offering feedback and pointing out choices. You do the rest. I hope that you will enjoy working with the material in the book, and that it will assist you on your vocal journey, whether as performer, teacher or coach.

SECTION 1

How the Voice Works

Chapters 1–4 deal with the how and why of your voice. Our instrument is inside us, and this makes our voice both exciting and mysterious. This might account for a residual fear among some trainers and performers of thinking 'too much' about what is happening when we sing and speak. Until relatively recently in our artistic history vocal trainers have had to rely on an empirical understanding of the voice. Both voice and medical science have made enormous strides in the last century, and we are now beginning to understand more about how the muscles work during singing and speaking, and how singers achieve some of the sounds they are able to make.

Singing is a physical skill, so you will find that most topics in the book are accompanied by something practical to do. The awareness exercises in Chapters 1–4 are particularly important, laying a foundation for work in the rest of the book. These exercises will help beginners to 'find' the muscles of their voice and more experienced singers to gain finer control. Both groups will benefit from the greater understanding that, in my experience, leads to a more confident performer.

Vowels used in the vocal exercises throughout the book are from simple vowels of General British. This has been a conscious decision on my part to avoid confusion between vowel placement and vocal production that might be dependent on Italian vowels. The intention is that the remaining simple and compound vowels can be included as and when needed. Those coming from different language bases may wish to adapt the exercises to include vowels more standard to their own speech. However, it is worth bearing in mind that, if you plan to sing Musical Theatre repertoire in the original language, then, for the most part, you will need to consider mastering the vowels of General British English and American.

Phonetic symbols are used for the first time in Chapter 4. This is for the sake of clarity in making some of the sounds used in the exercises. Whenever a phonetic symbol is used in the book, it appears with an interpretive spelling. You will find a list of these spellings alongside their IPA symbols at the beginning of Chapter 5 on pages 42–4. Thereafter phonetics feature regularly in the text.

Chapter 1

How do I make the notes?

Recently I gave a first lesson to a bright, intelligent, professional actress who had trained for three years at a Drama College. 'I really don't know how to sing,' she told me. 'I think I've got a voice and I can read music, but I don't know how to make the notes.'

So how do you make the notes? In this chapter we shall be looking at the nature of the vocal instrument: its physical and acoustic properties and what these mean for the singer who 'plays' the instrument. The topics for discussion will include the tube of the vocal tract, the larynx and the vocal folds. There are also awareness exercises to put you in touch with the different parts of the mechanism, so that you can feel as well as understand what is being discussed.

THE VOCAL MECHANISM

The vocal tract

Look at Diagram 1. Your voice, or vocal tract, is a kind of pipe. At the bottom end, inside the neck, it is relatively narrow. At the top end it opens out into the mouth and nasal cavity.

The whole vocal tract is a resonator. You can test this by holding your breath and flicking your finger against the side of your neck near the larynx. The sound will be hollow. If you then mouth vowel sounds you can hear how the vocal tract shapes itself differently for each one, even without you introducing any voicing.

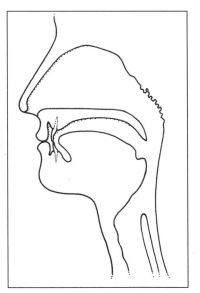

Diagram 1: the vocal mechanism

The larynx and vocal folds

The larynx is at the top of the windpipe, and forms the housing of the vocal folds. This is where sound is initiated. The larynx is a vibrator. This is important because a resonator on its own cannot generate sound; it can only amplify and shape it. Just as some wind instruments have a reed, your voice has two vocal folds that vibrate to produce sound. The vocal folds must move closer together to generate sound. A rapid closing and opening of the vocal folds produces the 'sound signal'. Here is an exercise to give you a sense of what is meant by vocal fold vibration.

Awareness exercise 1: THE VIBRATING MECHANISM

1. Blow breath gently through your lips; they should be almost closed. You will get an airy sound without pitch.
2. Start to blow a little harder and regulate the pressure until you produce a 'lip trill'. This is similar to the sound signal produced by the vocal folds at the level of the larynx before it is shaped by the resonator. Notice what you needed for this task:
i. You needed breath to excite the vibration of the lips;
ii. You needed to regulate the breath pressure for efficient vibrations – in singing and speaking we call this sub-glottic pressure;
iii. You needed something that could vibrate: the lips or vocal folds.

Now explore what happens if we introduce vibrations at the larynx, using the vocal tract as a sound shaper.
3. Make the lip-trill again. This time, introduce voicing as you do it. You can do this by thinking of humming behind the lip trill. If you place your fingers on your larynx you will feel vibration there as you start the 'hum'.

Notice that for this task, both the lips and the vocal folds are vibrating, and the vocal tract is shaping the sound.

MAKING THE NOTES

For good singing, you need airflow, vocal fold closure, and effective use of the resonators:

Function of the instrument:	**Power**	**Source**	**Filter**
Where it happens:	Lungs	Larynx	Vocal tract
Singing terminology:	Breath	Tone	Resonance

Diagram 2 shows where these are in the vocal tract. Later we will look at these structures and the muscle groups involved.

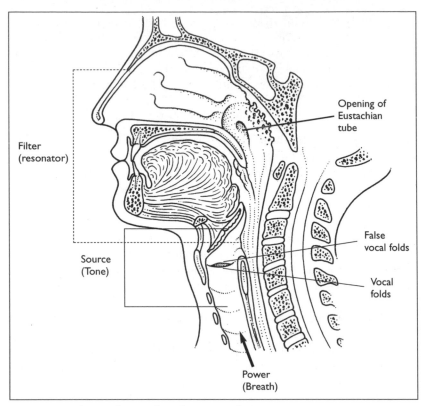

Diagram 2: the vocal tract; breath, tone and resonator

When you sing middle C, the vocal folds are closing and opening approximately 262 times a second. Various complex forces enable this to happen: aerodynamic, muscular and elastic forces in the larynx. Your vocal folds are not 'passive' in the act of phonation (making sound). They are actively chopping up the breath stream to form little pulses of air. A train of these small puffs of air pressure makes up the sound source. The sound source is then picked up by the tube of the vocal tract and modified according to its size and shape. A unique feature of the voice is that the shape of the vocal tract can be varied to produce different sound qualities. No other acoustic instrument can do this at will. Each vocalist is blessed with a personal graphic equaliser!

Sound production: the basics

The pitch (the note that you sing) is determined by the number of times your vocal folds close and open per second. This is called the fundamental frequency. When you sing a note, the vocal folds also produce a range of other frequencies above the fundamental. These other frequencies are called overtones or harmonics. Let's look at the harmonics that occur when you sing the fundamental frequency on the note C two octaves below middle C (65 Hertz or vibrations per second.)

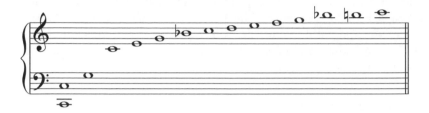

You'll hear other harmonics as part of the individual note that is being made. They contribute to sound quality. All acoustic instruments are recognisable by their individual sound quality, due to the groups of harmonics favoured by their shape. (Listen to a violin, a flute, a clarinet and trumpet playing the same note; they all sound different). Knowing how the voice works as an acoustic instrument is of positive benefit to you as a singer. As an actor you already have an instinctive awareness of acoustics because you are used to changing your vocal production for working in different acoustic spaces. You are also used to thinking about resonance and projection. We do not always stop to think about our voice as an instrumentalist does – from inside.

Here is a summary of the basics of sound production. You need:

1. Efficient vocal fold closure to produce a strong fundamental frequency. This contributes to the sense of ease in the sound.

2. Balanced energy in the harmonics. This will give your voice depth of quality and contribute to projection.

3. Breath pressure for the vocal folds to sustain vibrations.

Each voice has the same component parts; that is why we can *all* sing. However, shapes and sizes of the vocal tract vary as much as our body shapes, so each voice will be unique.

'Head' and 'chest' voice: myth or fact?

You may be looking at the power-source-filter diagram (Diagram 2) and wondering about head and chest voice. These are terms that I do not use except in relation to a student's previous training. They are ancient terms relating to physical sensations, which can lead inexperienced singers into thinking that they have somehow to 'join' two separate voices. These physical sensations of the sound being made or placed in the head and chest arise from sympathetic vibrations, from bone conduction and sometimes from muscular effort. It is more accurate to refer to head and chest 'registers'. Rather like the patches on an electronic keyboard, your voice has definable registers. These are usually different in sound quality and may be associated with different parts of your range. Hence we talk about register changes and register 'breaks'. We will be looking at why and how these happen in later chapters, as well as how to manage them. For now, I would like you take the idea of 'head and chest voice', wrap it beautifully and put it to one side. You will discover more helpful ways of dealing with these mechanical changes in your voice, as well as with changes of quality, as we go along.

Practice exercises

Here are a series of exercises to put you in touch with your instrument: how it feels and sounds, and how you might visualise the parts inside moving. With many of the exercises in the book I shall be giving you cues to help you in your learning. Diagrams and imagery are visual cues. Comments such as 'it may sound like' are auditory cues. Comments such as 'notice how it feels' and 'it feels as if' are kinaesthetic cues. Use the cues that work best for you.

Awareness exercise 2: CLOSING THE VOCAL FOLDS

1. Make a sound of friendly caution: 'uh-oh'. The sound should be crisp and clear and the feeling unforced. A small glottal stop precedes each of the vowel sounds. You might like to visualise the stop by bringing your hands close together and giving two short claps in time with the sound.
2. Repeat the sound several times in spoken voice. Keep it simple; this is an everyday sound used in many languages.
3. Now go to make the sound again, but stop just before you do it. Notice that the breath is stopped when you do this. (If you are using your hands you might like to hold them closed.)
   Focus on any sensations you have in your larynx. Can you feel the stop there? Listen to any noise that comes out when you release the stop. You will probably hear a little pop of air when you release the stop. That is the sound of the glottis (the space between the two vocal folds) opening and letting the breath out.

The aim of this exercise was to get you to feel where the sound began – in the larynx at the vocal folds. Even without making sound, you were able to control the breath by holding it back with your vocal folds. This is the closure that I referred to on page 3 – the 'sound source'. Breath was also needed for the vocal folds to close against. This relationship between vocal folds and breath is an essential part of good vocalising. You could blow air through the larynx and not bring the vocal folds together; this would just produce a noise of air in your vocal tract. Vocal fold closure is needed to produce sound.

'Sirening' and the soft palate

Another key area in which to develop awareness is the soft palate. The soft palate can filter the sound, sending it out through the nose, or through the mouth, or both together. It plays an important role in resonating quality.

Awareness exercise 3: LOCATING THE SOFT PALATE

1. Breathe gently in and out through your nose. Open your lips and continue to breathe through the nose. Focus attention on your tongue and where you can feel it in your mouth.
2. Now say the word 'sing', making the 'ng' at the end last longer than the vowel. You may become aware that your tongue is touching something at the back of your mouth in making this sound, just as when you were breathing in and out through your nose. This is your soft palate or velum.
3. Now say 'ing-ing-ing-ing-ing', keeping your mouth still and hardly moving your tongue. You may find it helpful to look in a mirror to make sure your movements are minimal.
   Do you feel something moving as you make this sound? If you are not sure what is moving, try out the following:
4. Make the consonant 'k' with medium hard pressure. This is a stopped consonant, so your breath will be first held and then released. Focus on the movement you feel when the breath is released with the sound 'k'. Your palate stays up against the back wall of your vocal tract and the tongue drops away from it.
5. Now repeat stages 1–3 focusing on the location of your soft palate.

Let's now explore the vocal mechanism further by sirening. This exercise has been described as 'listening with your muscles' and will give you awareness of how physical effort levels change as you move through your vocal range.

Awareness exercise 4: THE SIREN

This exercise takes its title from the sound of an emergency vehicle with its siren sounding, where the pitch is sliding up and down quite rapidly.

Unlike a real-life siren, this exercise is performed quietly.

1. Start by making the 'ng' sound as in the previous exercise (think of the word 'sing'). Your tongue should be raised at the back, and spread at the sides so that it is touching the upper back molars.
2. Imagine the sound of a small puppy whining and whimpering. Imitate these sounds using the 'ng'. Do this as quietly as you can, using very little breath.
3. Now begin to make a larger excursion with your siren, doing the pitch-glide in larger and larger loops like this:

4. Finally, make the siren from the bottom to the top of your vocal range. Pay attention to any changes you feel and hear.
i. The siren may not feel equally easy all the way up and down. This is what we call a change in effort level.
ii. Your voice may 'crack' or disappear at certain points in your range. Many people refer to this as a register 'break'.
   Both these experiences are common and are, in fact, normal.

Your vocal folds are tensed in order to vibrate faster for the high notes. They may also be lengthened. Both factors mean increased work in the larynx. On the lower notes, the vocal fold muscles will relax again and will be vibrating more slowly. Some people have difficulty managing these changes, leading to unevenness in the sound. This crack or break in the voice can easily be remedied. Constriction in the larynx can also occur as a panic reaction to these changes in the vocal folds, causing the voice to cut out completely. If you are experiencing these problems now, don't worry, as I will give you strategies to fix them in Chapters 5 and 7.

Let's finish with some monitoring devices for the siren:

1. Breath use
How much breath do you need to make the whimpering noises? Aim to match this when you are doing the full siren. Note that I am talking about how much breath you used *to make the sound*, rather than how much you took in. Find out if you can tailor your breath intake to the sound. (Remember to do the siren quietly.)

2. Head, neck and jaw posture

i. Notice what is happening with the back of your neck when you make the full siren. You might be 'reaching' for the high notes by raising the chin and pushing downwards with the chin as you go down again. Aim to straighten and lengthen the back of your neck at difficult points of the siren.

ii. Look in a mirror to see what you are doing with your jaw. Notice if you are opening the jaw very widely for the extreme ends of your range. Explore sirening with a smaller jaw position.

3. The vocal tract

Focus attention on the tongue and soft palate inside your mouth. Where is your tongue positioned? Can you feel your soft palate and upper back molars with your tongue? Does the tongue want to move away from the soft palate as you go up in pitch? Aim to keep the tongue and palate together throughout the siren, using the same position as in whimpering and whining.

It is easy for singers and their teachers to become very sound-focused. I call this aiming for outcome instead of adjusting the input. By working with these awareness exercises you will develop a feel for which muscle groups are working both before and as you make the sound. This in turn will give you greater control and will improve your confidence. Keep 'listening'!

Chapter 2

My voice won't come out at auditions

It is the morning of an important audition. You are well rehearsed and know that you are capable of delivering a good performance, but the situation makes you feel nervous and excited. Adrenalin is rushing round your body, your pulse is racing, and there are butterflies in your stomach. You open your mouth to sing, and everything seizes up! You keep singing, but, for some reason, your voice does not feel the same as usual. In fact, it feels like your voice is trapped in your throat, and you do not sound like yourself. You leave the audition wondering what happened. This is a common experience, and it can happen to both 'singers' and actors who sing.

In this chapter we shall be looking at why the larynx constricts and what to do about it, and how to coordinate breath and tone. Mastering these techniques will prepare you for the more advanced work in this book and will enable you to rely on your voice in auditions.

The larynx and primary function

In order to survive, the body is equipped with certain programmes of primary functioning. The larynx's primary function is to protect our airways, stopping saliva and food particles from getting into the lungs. Essentially the larynx is a sphincter mechanism. The larynx also has a secondary function, which is to act as a pressure valve. By closing off the airway, the larynx enables us to strain, give birth and vomit. The pressure valve also enables us to clear the lungs when we need to cough.

Speech and singing are learned behaviours and came later in our evolution than the instinctive functions above. The tendency of the larynx to close up is therefore part of a protective programming that is perfectly natural. Laryngeal constriction can also be triggered by psychological factors, such as the flight and fight mechanism. Simplistic though it may sound, your larynx does not know the difference between an audition situation and one of actual physical threat. The chemical response in your body is the same.

How can we overcome constriction in performance situations?

LARYNGEAL CONSTRICTION AND RELEASE

The diagrams below show the vocal folds viewed from above. Notice that there are two sets of folds, shown in two different positions.

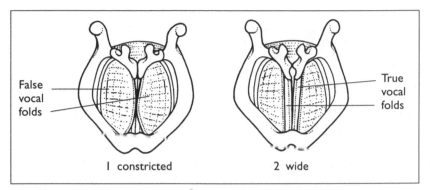

The false vocal folds: diagram 1 – constricted, and diagram 2 – retracted

The shaded area represents the false vocal folds. The false vocal folds can cause problems in singing and speaking by closing up the airspace above the true folds. This disturbance upsets vocal fold vibration and can either contaminate the sound or stop it from coming out altogether. This is what we mean by 'constriction'.

Notice that in Diagram 1, you can really see only the false vocal folds, which have almost closed over the true vocal folds. In Diagram 2, you can see the true vocal folds more clearly because the false folds have moved out of the way. If you would like to visualise where the false folds fit into the whole vocal tract, refer to page 4, where they are indicated on Diagram 2. You can see that the true and false vocal folds are very close to each other, with the false folds above the true folds in the vocal tract.

Here are two exercises to develop awareness of the false vocal folds and their effect on vocalising:

Awareness exercise 1: CONSTRICTION

The false folds are naturally constricted when we are straining or grunting.
1. From a sitting position, lift your feet off the ground so that they are not supporting any weight.
2. Place both hands under the chair and try to lift you and the chair off the ground. Notice what is happening in the larynx: the false folds will constrict as you work harder to pull yourself up.

What's the sensation? Do you feel something pushing down and in, inside your throat, and the air pushing up from your abdomen? This is the feeling of constriction.

Awareness exercise 2: RETRACTION

1. Think of a funny situation that makes you want to smile inside. Hold the feeling of that inner smile.
2. Allow the sensation of the inner smile to develop further down in your vocal tract. Let it move from the inside of the mouth down to the inside of your neck where the larynx is.
3. Add sound to the feel of inner smile, allowing yourself to giggle or chuckle.
4. Let the sensation grow into laughing. Laughing out loud on 'hee- hee', 'hah-hah' or 'ho-ho', whatever works for you.
5. Now visualise being in a silent movie. Laugh silently, working just as hard as you did before.
6. As you continue to laugh silently, notice the physical work involved. Where do you feel it? To help you monitor these sensations of effort, give them an effort number – a score between one and ten. What is your effort number when you laugh silently?

Monitoring your effort
Holding the feeling of silent laughing may be effortful. Use the following checklist to release extraneous tensions in the body while maintaining your effort number in the silent laugh:

i. Breathe in and out gently and freely, with no bouncing of the abdominal wall!

ii. Chew lazily with your jaw and roll your tongue around inside your mouth.

iii. Massage your face until the laugh is no longer visible on the outside.

iv. Check your general posture as you walk around the room freely and easily.

Remembering the effort number of your silent laugh will help you to embed the muscle memory of retraction. Keep holding this effort number while releasing other tensions above.

Do you feel a new sense of space in your larynx? That is the feeling of retraction. Notice how hard you were working in the exercise. Retracted is not the same as relaxed. Notice that it is more difficult to remain retracted when other muscles come into play. If you like, repeat stages 4–6 from the previous awareness exercise, and then gently sing a note on the vowel 'EE'. Notice how it feels and sounds. When I work this exercise with clients, they – particularly the 'non-singers' – are often surprised at the sounds they can make. A well-trained vocalist will normally be retracted in the larynx already and recognise the sensation. Those who have sung very little often need to work at maintaining the retracted position because they are not used to sustaining pitch.

Not everybody gets the idea of the silent laugh at first. There are so many different sensations associated with laughter that it is easy to confuse them and not achieve false fold retraction. Here is another route to retraction that you will find helpful if this applies to you.

Awareness exercise 3: AUDITORY MONITORING USING SILENT BREATHING

1. Sitting in a relaxed position, breathe in and out through your mouth as if asleep.
2. Put your fingers in your ears and listen to the sound inside your head. (Some people hear more on the out-breath, others more on the in-breath.)
3. Keeping your fingers in the ears, continue to breathe in and out, allowing the sound of the breath to decrease gradually. You can use one hand to check that you are still breathing (place one hand on the abdomen or close up against the mouth to feel the out-breath).
4. Continue until there is no sound at all inside your head. Make sure you are gently breathing throughout. This is the retracted position.
5. What is your number now on the scale of effort?
   Repeat stages 1–4, and then sing a note.

Do you need to use retraction all the time? Mostly, yes. In everyday speech and for relaxed voice qualities, you do not need to be retracted; you simply need to avoid constriction. For projected singing and high-energy voice qualities such as opera and belting, retraction is a must. It enables a wide and free movement of the vocal folds during vibration. Perform the exercises a few times until you can feel for yourself where the constriction is made and released. There will be more work on retraction in Chapter 5.

EFFORT AND AWARENESS

In dealing with laryngeal constriction we have targeted one of the main issues that will preoccupy you as a performer – how to appear real without tension patterns making themselves known in performance. Singing is a complex vocal task, involving pitching, moving the larynx, aerodynamic control and physical energy. Here is an exercise in awareness of effort.

Awareness exercise 4: MONITORING PERSONAL EFFORT

Use a soft ball or something similar for this exercise.
1. Hold the ball in one hand. Move your arm around, getting in touch with the weight and size of the ball, until you feel comfortable holding it.
2. Give that feeling a number on the scale of effort.
3. Now squeeze the ball with your hand and give that feeling a number.
4. Keep squeezing the ball with the same effort level while you wave your other hand around in the air.
5. Keep squeezing the ball, while you wave your other hand and talk out loud.
6. Keep squeezing and waving, and make a siren, keeping the sound quiet and small.

It is important for this exercise that you continue squeezing the ball *with the same effort level* throughout.

Make a note of what changed for you during the exercise. It is common to lose the effort in the squeeze when you either relax other structures in the body, such as waving the other hand around, or when you introduce more complex tasks. Experiment further with other effort levels in the 'squeeze factor', working with a ball in each hand and doing more complex vocal tasks such breathing exercises or singing songs.

In monitoring personal effort you need to find out where you are working and how hard. You need to isolate the muscles used in tasks and to decide what is appropriate to the task. Use the *Isolation Checklist* to check your effort levels. It will enable you to engage physical effort in a controlled manner for work in later chapters.

ISOLATION CHECKLIST

Release the abdominal wall so that you can breathe in and out easily, using voiced fricatives or walking around.
Silently laugh at the larynx to retract the false vocal folds.
Chew freely with the jaw.
Roll the tongue around inside the mouth.
Speak softly on vowel sounds and/or siren through your range to isolate voicing from bigger muscular tasks.

We are now going to complete the work in this chapter by exploring the relationship between breath and tone.

CONTROLLING ONSET OF TONE

The start or onset of a note can be a difficult moment for an inexperienced singer. The glottis (the space between the vocal folds) must close for sound to be produced, so controlling onset of tone requires you to coordinate breath with glottal closure. As you do the following exercises you might feel as though the tone starts in different places. Be aware of what is happening with the breath, and listen out for any changes in tonal quality.

Awareness exercise 5: THE GLOTTAL ONSET

The auditory cues for this onset are the 'uh-oh' from Awareness Exercise 2 from Chapter 1 (page 6), and the 'ah' of realisation. Check that you are retracted when you do these so that there is no danger of constriction.
1. Make either sound, but stop just before you actually make the sound. The breath will be held by the true vocal folds.
2. Keeping your folds together say 'EE' as you release into the sound. Notice that, at the same time, you will let the breath come through as well.
3. Say 'EE' a few times like this, and then start to pitch it on a note in a comfortable part of your voice.
4. Repeat this exercise with other vowel sounds.

In a glottal onset, the glottis is closed before the onset of tone and release of breath. The glottal onset used here is not the same as a hard glottal attack. Notice that there will be a distinct 'edge' at the start of each note and that the breath stops each time before you make the sound.

Awareness exercise 6: THE ASPIRATE ONSET

The auditory cues for this onset are the hooting of an owl or the word 'Hey'!
1 Aim to initiate tone with the breath, using an 'h' before the vowel 'h-OO'.
2. Bring your hand close up to your mouth to feel the air on your hand before the tone begins.
3. Repeat stages 1-2, substituting other vowel sounds after the 'h'.

With the aspirate onset, the breath is released before tone causing the glottis to close. Notice that this time there is no stop and that the work is in the breath. You will also hear an 'h' before each vowel.

Awareness exercise 7: THE SIMULTANEOUS ONSET

The auditory cues for this onset are a whining child ('Oh, please, mummy') or a moaning adult ('Oh dear').

1. Take in a small breath and hold your vocal folds open (check this by silently breathing out again).
2. Make a small moaning sound on 'oh' or 'yes' (breathe in again if you need to first).
3. Repeat the 'oh' a few times, aiming to hold the breath with the vocal folds open between each initiation of tone. Alternatively, repeat the 'yes' a few times until you can leave out the 'y' and make the onset just on 'EE'. Aim to hold the breath and vocal folds open between each initiation of tone as above.
4. Repeat stages 1-3 with all vowels.

With the simultaneous onset, the glottis closes in time with the release of breath, so the tone happens 'simultaneously'. You may notice a more controlled release of breath, almost as if it is held when you start the note. You voice may feel as though it is coming from a different place.

There is more than one way to begin tone. In each of the above onsets the vocal folds were coming together against the breath yet the outcome was different. None of them is incorrect, and they are all used in singing. Many people have an habitual onset that they use in singing or speaking and are unaware of how this can affect their vocal efficiency. By practising the different onsets you will be able to differentiate between them. This will give you more choice as a performer.

Chapter 3

But I thought I wasn't supposed to feel anything!

This chapter is about discovering subtle movements of the larynx. If you can learn how your larynx moves you are less likely to be limited by your own habitual vocal patterns. Your physical training as an actor is geared towards strength, flexibility and expression. Why should it be any different with your voice? Using exercises to refine movements of the larynx will help you to develop a flexible instrument, capable of a broad emotional range and subtlety of nuance.

Traditionally in vocal training (both singing and speaking), the student is discouraged from focusing on their larynx. In singers this can lead to dependency on the vocal teacher; in actors it can breed insecurity. Despite significant advances in voice science, a Victorian attitude towards our larynx persists in pedagogy, as though it is wrong to feel anything 'down there'! There is also a fear that preoccupation with the mechanical aspect of singing will inhibit artistic expression. Both must be developed to train creative performers.

You need to know your instrument. Many singers rely totally on auditory feedback to monitor their singing. Your instrument is inside you, and you cannot hear it accurately. It is good to develop other sensory feedback. One client came to me with his voice in trouble. He had already tried a number of different teachers, but his voice problems persisted. He clearly had a wonderful instrument but was running into vocal difficulties because he was overworking his vocal folds. One day I heard him sirening a song as he stood outside my front door, waiting for me to answer. In fact I had been able to hear him approaching the house from several houses away. Hearing the sound from him that I had been working to get for the last few lessons, I set to work on identifying the feel of what he called 'singing to himself'. It turned out that, only when he was singing loudly, did he get the auditory feedback he relied on to tell him that he was singing well. He could not believe that his small siren carried so well. By separating feel from sound, he was able to develop a more reliable technique.

LARYNGEAL ORIENTEERING: A SHORT COURSE

During singing it is not always easy to monitor what is happening with the larynx. For this reason, many of the awareness exercises that I give to clients to develop sensory feedback are done without sound or using noises. Let's start by considering how we can develop awareness of the larynx.

Awareness exercise 1: GENERAL AWARENESS

Think about a part of your body – say – your big toe. How do you know it is there? Can you feel it just by putting your attention on it, or do you need to look at it? Or move it? Probably you wriggled your toe inside your shoe or sock in order to check that it was there. But if there had been no shoe or sock, and if you hadn't moved the big toe, how did you know it was actually there?

How do you feel your larynx? When are you aware of it? There are three ways to feel the larynx:
1. by swallowing (as it moves);
2. by vocalising (you will feel it when it vibrates);
3. by feeling it from outside by touch.
Let's explore the last possibility further.

Feeling the larynx, 'hands on'

People may be wary of touching the larynx, and I would certainly agree that, unless you are in the hands of a professional such a speech therapist, an osteopath or an ENT surgeon, it is only advisable to do this yourself. It is natural to feel vulnerable in the area where we give voice to our feelings. However, I encourage my own clients to self-monitor their larynx. Many of them find it useful, and none of them has come to harm.

Awareness exercise 2: FEELING THE LARYNX

Look at the photograph and Diagram 1 on page 20 before you start. The latter shows you the anatomical parts of the larynx in an exploded view; the photograph shows where to position your hands for external monitoring.

1. Your larynx is between the two big muscles on the side of the neck. Locate the top of these by putting one or two fingers behind each ear (mastoid process) and work downwards, following the course of the muscles in a narrowing 'V' shape. As you reach the underneath of your chin, move inside the 'V' a little way until you can feel something harder than muscle. This will be your hyoid bone.

Feeling the larynx.

2. Notice that the bone is free-floating and that it is shaped like a horseshoe. The bone seems to be nestling amid dense muscle. These are the muscles that make up the floor of the mouth.
3. Swallow and notice what happens. There is a strong 'kicking' movement from these muscles when you swallow, and the hyoid bone moves upwards and forwards.
4. Continue moving down, using gentle contact with both fingers. You will go through a soft area and then come to another harder structure. This is the thyroid cartilage.

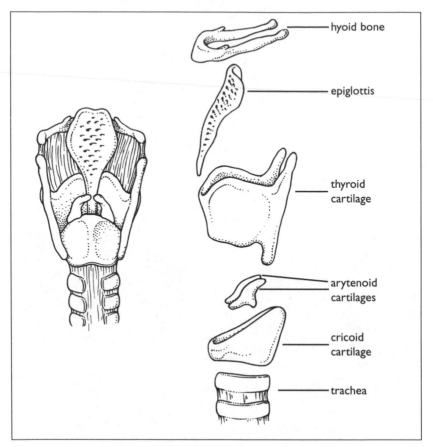

Diagram 1: Cartilages of the larynx – exploded view; after Sundberg.

5. Feel around for the sides of the thyroid cartilage and sense its width. If you look at the anatomical diagram you can see its shape is rather like a shield that is open at the back.

6. Narrowing in and down just a little further, you will come to the cricoid cartilage. You may feel a very small dip between it and the thyroid above. The cricoid may feel like a little lump of cartilage, and it sits on top of your windpipe. If you swallow again, it will move up with the rest of your larynx. The cricoid and the thyroid together house the vocal folds. Together with the hyoid bone and the epiglottis shown on the left of Diagram 2, they make up the larynx.

You might like to look at the Diagram 2 of the whole vocal tract to see where these structures fit into the instrument as a whole.

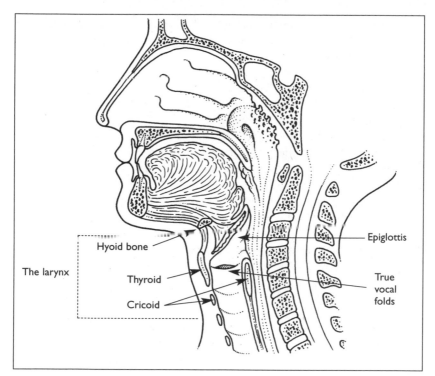

Diagram 2: The vocal tract

Moving the larynx

The exercises that follow should be done first without external monitoring. They will enable you to become aware of a range of movement that is normal in a healthy larynx.

Awareness exercise 3: RAISING AND LOWERING YOUR LARYNX

1. Raise your larynx by making a small squeak or siren on a high pitch. The larynx naturally rises with high pitches.
2. Lower your larynx by doing a 'yawn-sigh' manoeuvre. Start off on a yawn and sigh out as you finish. Most people breathe in deeply as they yawn, and this will tend to lower the larynx.

Awareness exercise 4: MOVING THE LARYNX FORWARDS AND BACKWARDS

1. Go into the posture of someone about to whine or whimper. The thyroid cartilage of the larynx will move forwards.

2. Now start to swallow, stopping near the beginning of your swallow as though something is stuck on its way down. Your larynx will move a little way backwards.

Monitoring for awareness exercises 3 and 4
Using the following modes of monitoring will help you embed muscle memory for these movements.

i. Go through the movements again while feeling the larynx from the outside as shown in the photograph on page 19. Don't worry if the movements are small; they are subtle. You are now using external monitoring to help develop a kinaesthetic awareness of your larynx.

ii. If you are a visual learner you may find it helpful to work with a partner, or to look in a mirror. Some of these movements (not all) can be seen from outside.

iii.If you are an auditory learner, you might like to find the postures and then speak out loud in them. Explore speaking on a range of different pitches in any of these modes. Listening to the difference in sound will help you remember the 'feel'.

iv. Make a note of changes in effort levels as you move your larynx into the different positions.

The inexperienced singer will often change posture in the neck in order to achieve extremes of the range. It is difficult to feel 'high' and 'low' and so we tend to try to do it from the outside. Some singers will put their chins down to get low notes and lift up to get the high ones. Remind yourself that pitch is made in the larynx and that you can aid this process by keeping your head and neck in alignment.

A healthy larynx has a good range of movement up and down. When you alter your larynx position you will change your voice quality. A shorter vocal tract (high larynx) will favour the higher harmonics and give a brighter sound; a longer vocal tract (low larynx) will favour the lower harmonics and give a darker sound. Neither of these positions is wrong unless the larynx is fixed there.

Postures of the larynx

In addition to movement up and down, the larynx has other postures that are particularly relevant to voice use in singing.

Look at Diagrams 3–5 of the thyroid and cricoid cartilages and notice that there are three different positions.

1. *Neutral or rest position.* This is how the larynx is best positioned for both everyday and theatre speaking voice. It will enable you to access the lower part of your range with a strong direct sound.

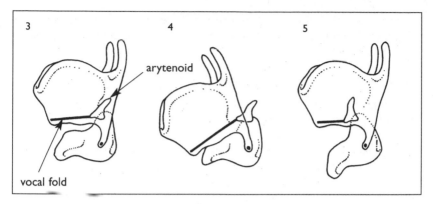

The thyroid and cricoid cartilages: diagram 3 – neutral or rest position, diagram 4 – forward tilt of the thyroid cartilage, and diagram 5 – forward tilt of the cricoid cartilage.

2. *Forward tilt of the thyroid cartilage.* This position enables the vocal folds to be lengthened and tensioned for higher pitches. You will have difficulty accessing your upper range if you do not do this forward tilting. Finding this tilted posture can also help you in creating vibrato if you want it.[1] Because this position stretches the vocal folds, it is important to release it for everyday speech.

3. *Forward tilt of the cricoid cartilage.* This is a change of posture required for safe belting. The diagram shows the cricoid moving forward of the thyroid, so that the vocal folds are shortened[2].

Awareness exercise 5: TILTING THE THYROID

1. Imagine the sound of a whining child or the whimpering of a puppy. If this doesn't suit you, moan gently. The sound has to be high(ish) in pitch, but don't try to sing. Just make the noise. Most people can do this after a little practice.
2. Just as we did with the glottal onset and silent laugh in earlier chapters, make the movement without the sound. This posture can feel quite effortful if you are not used to it. Make sure you are retracted so that you can avoid constriction. This is the forward tilt of the thyroid.

This is one of the more subtle movements of the larynx. Sometimes, during a class, I will ask a client to feel for the thyroid tilting on my larynx.

[1] There are other ways to access vibrato, but this is the one I use the most with my clients.
[2] Or the thyroid has moved backwards and upwards of the cricoid: there is no agreement yet among researchers.

They will often comment on how small the movement is. You may well find it easier to feel this type of tilting by comparing it with the neutral position:

Awareness exercise 6: MOVING FROM NEUTRAL TO TILTED THYROID

1. Breathe out using voiced fricatives such as 'v' and 'z'. Do this on a low pitch. Put your fingers on the larynx if you like to feel the vibrations there.
2. Now make a glottal onset using the sound 'uh-oh', still on a low pitch. Put your fingers on your larynx as before, or use visual monitoring as described earlier.
3. Now make the sound of the whine or moan.
4. Repeat the movement without the sound.
5. Keep alternating between the voiced fricatives followed by the glottal onset, and the silent whine or moan. Eventually you will identify a change in posture.

Awareness exercise 7: TILTING THE CRICOID

You are going to take an upper chest breath.
1. Put a hand on your breastbone and feel the breath coming into the chest as you gasp in surprise. (This will also help you to raise the larynx.)
2. Make a small squeak on the vowel 'EE' keeping the silent laugh at all times. The auditory cue is of a tiny mouse squeaking. The sound should not be loud.

Probably you have tilted the cricoid in this manoeuvre. This type of tilting is more difficult to isolate, but you need to know that it exists and that it is a necessary part of the set-up for safe belting. We shall look at tilting the cricoid in more detail in Chapter 12.

Don't worry that I have asked you to do two things that are normally considered to be poor technique in singing, i.e. taking an upper chest breath and making a squeak. Your voice is capable of many things, and both these actions can be performed safely if you have awareness and are able to retract the false vocal folds.

Applications
Raising and lowering the larynx will change the length of the vocal tract tube. This will change your resonating quality. The deeper tones of a lowered larynx are preferred by some schools of teaching and are desirable as part of the set-up for the operatic voice. However, this is an aesthetic consideration, not one of vocal health; it is not necessary to lower the larynx for healthy voicing. A high larynx is essential for some of

the voice qualities currently used in musical theatre – notably twang and belt. Raising the larynx will also give you easier access to the notes at the top of your range.

Tilting the larynx has various uses. You will generally find it easier to negotiate your first main gear change by engaging thyroid tilt. This posture is also used in classical and 'legit' singing. Conversely, you need to release the thyroid tilt to get to the bottom of your range, where the vocal folds like to be shorter and thicker; you also need this position for more contemporary musical theatre and pop vocal styles. Tilting the cricoid will help you negotiate your gear change in an alternative way to thyroid tilt and will be useful in helping you to find your 'belt' notes.

Vocal fold postures

In the previous chapter we looked at three positions or postures for the false vocal folds. Here are two possible postures for the true vocal folds.

Look at Diagram 6 representing the vocal fold and arytenoid within the thyroid and cricoid cartilages. Notice that there are two positions of the vocal folds from front to back inside the cartilages; the black line shows the vocal folds lying horizontally and the dotted line shows them raised at the back. The arytenoid (shaped like a small pyramid) has moved backwards, pulling the back of the vocal fold with it.[3] Because of the way the arytenoids move, the vocal folds will not only

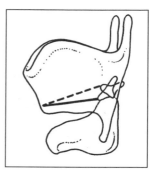

Diagram 6: The thyroid and cricoid cartilages – horizontal and raised plane positions of the vocal fold.

be raised at the back in this position, they will also be pulled open. As in thyroid tilting, you can see that the vocal fold is slightly longer in this position. The 'raised plane' position seems to be responsible for falsetto voice quality. Inexperienced singers will often find this raised plane position by default when they are going into their upper range.

Awareness exercise 8: CHANGING VOCAL FOLD PLANE

Here is an exercise to help you explore the raised and horizontal plane positions:
1. Start close to the bottom of your range and make a pitch-glide up using the word 'Hey'. Do this quite vigorously, and avoid modifying the sound or making any kind of adjustment as you go up in pitch.

[3] The movement of the arytenoids is actually more complex than described but beyond the scope of this book.

2. You will probably come to a point where it feels uncomfortably high and something needs to move. This is usually the point where the vocal fold plane will raise, and there will be a noticeable change of sound quality as something 'flips' up.
3. When the vocal fold plane alters you will probably feel a change in the breath and hear a change in the sound quality. This is raised plane position.
4. Now work from the other direction, starting quite high up in your range. Allow your breath to flow when you start off, as in sighing or vocalising a yawn.
5. Glide down in pitch towards the bottom of your range.
6. Once again, something may well seem to need to change position as you approach the low notes. It may feel like a push downwards. There will be a change in the breath and sound.
   This is horizontal plane position.

Notice that you are deliberately getting your voice to 'crack' when you do this. This is not the same as constriction. There is also a sensation that goes with the sound of the crack. Once again you are feeling something in your voice. Sometimes there is an audible pitch change too. Listen out for it.

Application
Many singers have been trained to avoid this flip or crack, but it is quite harmless. Negative practice is a useful tool, and if you have a crack or break in your voice it is best to find out where and what it is. In a similar manner to the tilting of the thyroid cartilage, the raised plane position gives a longer, somewhat thinner vocal fold, so it *is* a way to access higher pitches. (More of this in Chapter 7 when we discuss gear changes and their relationship to vocal registers.) In my teaching studio we refer to a rapid change of the vocal fold plane as 'flipping the plane'. This 'flip' is characteristic of yodelling, Country and Blue Grass Music, as well as some World Music, and it is currently used by some pop vocalists.

Learning to move the parts of the larynx and the larynx itself requires patience and application. While we do not have direct conscious control over these muscle groups, we can develop a muscle memory for them. The work in these first three chapters lays the foundations for some of the most important work in this book: developing the ability to change vocal set-up. Different configurations of the vocal folds and larynx allow us to create different voice qualities. These are invaluable tools of vocal expression, enabling you to act truthfully with your voice.

Chapter 4

What exactly is support?

'Your voice needs more support' is a common critique offered to singers. But what does it mean exactly? The word 'support' may be used very loosely to describe a number of different functions: it can mean airflow and breath management, or it can mean working muscles in the body to assist work in the vocal tract, or it can mean both. The aim of this chapter is to unravel some of the confusions about breath use and its role in supporting sustained vocal fold vibration. In Chapter 7 we will learn how to engage the body to assist the work done by the larynx and vocal folds.

PASSIVE RESPIRATION

In looking at passive respiration we can find out how the body is programmed to breathe for everyday life. We breathe in as a response to signals from the brain. The trigger for the signal is the need for oxygen. On receiving the signal the diaphragm contracts and pulls down, decreasing the air pressure in the chest so that the lungs fill with air. Other muscles also help by expanding the chest cavity; these are the muscles that raise the ribs and increase the width and depth of the ribcage. The diaphragm, however, is responsible for 60–80% of the work during inspiration.

When we breathe out, the diaphragm relaxes back to its normal, dome-like position, the chest cavity decreases, and air leaves the body. This is all that needs to happen during quiet respiration, and it happens automatically. You cannot support with or from the diaphragm; it is not active in expiration. Neither can you feel the diaphragm; you can feel only the effects of it contracting and drawing the air into the lungs.

When you breathe in, you will feel that your lower abdomen moves out as a result of the diaphragm pulling down. You will also feel the 5th to 12th ribs raising and your back expanding just where the ribcage ends. This is because the diaphragm is attached to the lower ribs and to the spine. All this happens automatically if you do not interfere with the functioning of the diaphragm. You need make no conscious effort to lift your ribs in order to draw air into the lungs.

When you breathe out, the space in your chest will decrease and your abdomen and ribs will return to their normal position.

It is a standard part of training for many actors to do release work enabling them to get in touch with their body and breath. For those who inhibit what is essentially a natural process, touching base with passive respiration is a good first step. However, singing and theatre voice work require a different awareness and a more energetic use of the muscles that will not feel 'relaxed'.

Phonation depends on the interruption of airflow. In passive breathing the cycles of inhalation and exhalation are roughly equal in length. Even for everyday speaking, the inhalation needs to be much faster and the exhalation slowed down. In singing the relationship between the breath cycles will alter further, with the exhalation being still more extended.

ACTIVE EXPIRATION

Singing requires an active use of the muscles involved in expiration. Some singing styles are less sustained than others, but the necessity to maintain pitch is common to all styles and voice qualities. This requires airflow and balanced air pressure. A range of muscle groups is available to us for use in active expiration. These include muscles of the chest, abdominal wall and the back. We shall be looking at some of these later in the chapter.

Three other factors affect our breath use in singing:

1. Changes in sub-glottic pressure.

This is the relationship between vocal fold resistance and the oncoming breath. Essentially your vocal folds act as a kind of valve mechanism. This means that they can affect the outflow of air. Since your vocal folds are also muscles, they have the ability to work harder or less hard in resisting the breath. This is bound to affect the outflow of air. This relationship between the flow of air and the pressure beneath the vocal folds is known as sub-glottic pressure.

2. Changes in voice quality.

Changes in the configuration of the vocal tract can also affect pressure and flow of breath. These configurations result in different voice qualities, and we shall be looking at some of them towards the end of the book. When the vocal folds are closed for longer during each cycle of vibration (as in belting), or when the tube of the larynx has been narrowed above the vocal folds (as in twang), there will be a change in air pressure and consequently in your breath use. Tongue positioning can also affect breath use, either causing air to back up in the vocal tract or allowing it to move freely onwards.

3. The demands of musical style and text.

Airflow needs to be appropriate to the singing task. The uninterrupted vocal line considered desirable in classical singing is not necessarily a requirement of other styles; jazz and pop singers, for example, will frequently articulate or accent their phrasing by breaking up the line. Consonants also interrupt and change the airflow. These include voiceless and voiced stops such as 'p' and 'b', and voiceless and voiced fricatives such as 'f' and 'v'. The former will stop the breath, and the latter will tend to demand more pressure in the breath and so use more air.

Understanding the role of these three features above is key, in my opinion, to good breath management.

Why breathing exercises?

Some singers are so fixated of breath 'control' that they do not breathe out enough. Others are tense either physically or psychologically and do not allow the breath to 'drop in'. These are really the only kind of mechanical breathing problems that people can have. Anything else, in my experience, arises from misunderstandings about what how we breathe or about what we might think 'should' happen when we breathe for singing. Explanations of muscle use and direction of effort will help you clarify how we breathe for singing; points 1–3 opposite will help you unravel misunderstandings about breath use.

Each of the exercises that follow has a specific purpose and is designed help you with your breath management. You can use them in conjunction with warm-up and song work. At the end of the chapter, there are some more advanced exercises for finding out how the breath behaves in different situations.

Breathing in: the elastic recoil

A very wise singing teacher told me during my training that the secret of breathing in was to breathe out. The exercises that follow are based on this principle and come from the Accent Method, first developed by Svend Smith[1]. The fricative consonants engage the muscles of active expiration, and they will help you to release the abdominal wall so that you can breathe in fast and efficiently. You can work the first exercise standing or sitting. Since it involves active use of the abdominal wall it is best not to do this exercise lying down.

Exercise 1: THE ELASTIC RECOIL

1. Put one hand over your abdomen. Your thumb should be roughly over your navel, with the rest of the hand lower down.

[1] Smith S, Thyme, K (1981). Die Akzentmethod, Vedbaek, Denmark, The Danish Voice Institute. Also Kotby MN, (1995) The Accent Method in Voice Therapy, San Diego, CA, Singular Pubs. Group Inc

2. Breathe out sharply on the sound 'PShhh'. Use your hand to send the abdomen right back towards your backbone. Don't bother to breathe in for this – you always have air in your lungs. Just concentrate on this energetic exhalation.
3. Notice that if you wait and allow your abdominal wall to relax at the end of the sound, the abdomen will bounce outwards and you will have breathed in. (For some people this 'bounce back' is actually quite slow to begin with, but it can be done quickly with practice.) Don't worry if this recoil breath didn't happen; as you continue with the exercise it will.
4. Repeat stages 2 and 3 a few times, until you feel that you are getting some movement inwards as you make the sound, and some movement outwards as you breathe in.

When our bodies are balanced and our movements coordinated, we are often aware of rhythm taking over. It's the same with the breath. Now work the following exercise.

Exercise 2: WORKING THE RECOIL WITH RHYTHM

1. Work with any or all of these voiceless fricatives: 'f', 'sh' /ʃ/, 's'. Make up a sequence with them, and start to build a comfortable rhythm as you breath in and out.
   Here are some example sequences using 'sh' /ʃ/:
   i.   Sh / Sh / Sh; take a breath between each sound;
   ii. sh-Sh / sh-Sh / sh-Sh; the letters in lower case here indicate upbeats; breathe between the pairs of sounds;
   iii. sh-Sh-Sh-Sh / sh-Sh-Sh-Sh; breathe after every four sounds.
   Remember that you breathe out on the sounds, sending your abdomen inwards, and you release your abdominal wall to recoil or breathe in.
2. You can work with these sounds in a variety of ways with different rhythms, using upbeats and as many main beats as you like. (An upbeat is the small beat before the main rhythmic stroke, like the unstressed syllable of the iambic metre.) When you do many repeated sounds on the out-breath, do not worry if your appear to do a part-recoil in-between; it doesn't matter. What is important is that the abdomen is moving inwards on each sound so that you can develop flexibility and muscularity of the abdominal wall.
   The voiceless fricatives help you to feel a build up of pressure against the airflow. However, make sure that you do not grip the jaw or lips as you make the sounds, as you will be making undue effort and might trigger constriction.
3. Repeats stages 1 and 2 with voiced fricatives: 'v', 'ge' /ʒ/, 'z'.

Pay attention to the following:

i. Fricatives are made with the breath, so you will feel effort at the point of obstruction (lips and tongue);

ii. With voiceless sounds ('f', 'sh' /ʃ/, 's'), you should feel nothing in the larynx because the vocal folds are not involved;

iii. With the voiced sounds you will feel more; you are forming the consonants in exactly the same way, but you will feel vibration in the lips ('v'), and tongue ('ge' /ʒ/, 'z') and in the larynx.

iv. With all of these voiced sounds you may also feel (and see, if you look in the mirror) your neck pulsating. This is fine; it is just your larynx vibrating as the vocal folds offer resistance to the oncoming air.

4. It is fun to add physical movement to this exercise to help you feel the direction of movement in the abdominal wall. Work stage 3 again, this time swaying backwards as you make the sound and forwards when you do the recoil breath.

This sequence can be practised in short bursts – about five minutes at a time is good – and it can form the beginning of a regular warm-up routine. Make sure that you have mastered the recoil before moving on to the advanced exercises that require more complex movements of the abdominal wall.

Addressing airflow: the diamond of support

The next series of exercises target the muscles of active expiration. They include work on the waistband or muscles of the abdominal wall, and they will enable you to address poor airflow. These exercises and the image of the 'diamond' are based on the work of Janice Chapman, and I, along with many other teachers and performers, am grateful for the work she has done and generously passed on in this field. I'd also like to acknowledge the work of Meribeth Dayme (formerly Bunch) for her insights into the mechanics of these exercises.

Awareness exercise I: THE WAISTBAND

1. Put your hands around your waistband at the sides; the thumbs should be going into the back of the waistband. Make sure you are working with the fleshy area between the bottom of your ribcage and the top of the pelvic crest. You are not feeling bone.

2. Cough quite gently. You will feel the muscles of the abdominal wall contract. You will experience this as a jump or push outwards of the muscles at either side of your waistband. The muscles will be contracting around the back, and also further down diagonally into the groin area.

3. Keeping your attention on the same area – the waistband and the muscles going into the groin – now voice a 'v' vigorously. Notice that the muscles will contract or jump outwards as they did in the cough. This will happen even though you are still sending the central section of your abdominal wall inwards towards the backbone as we were doing earlier to create airflow. The sensation of sending the abdomen inwards will not be as strong as before because you will be feeling a lateral pull as well. This is fine, so long as you know that your airflow is still there.

4. Now voice the 'v' several times in one breath, as if you were revving a motorcycle that has the accelerator on the handlebars. Notice that you can pulse with the abdominal wall more than once during a single expiration.

5. Repeat stage 4 using 'hey-hey' sounds instead of the voiced fricative.

This mixture of sensations in the abdominal wall is a source of confusion to many students: some believe that any tightening in the abdominal wall will prevent them from using their diaphragm; others believe that the 'support' comes from pushing the abdomen outwards at the centre. Keep your awareness on the following when vocalising:

1. the navel moves inwards;

2. the waistband moves laterally.

This lateral movement of the abdominal wall need not be engaged during inspiration; you need only engage these muscles when vocalising. If you use them during inspiration you may lock the body and the breath. Always release the abdominal wall, especially around the navel, when you have finished your phrase and want to breathe in. Look at Diagrams 1 and 2 to help you visualise the muscles you are working in Awareness exercises 2 and 3.

Awareness exercise 2: THE ABDOMINAL WALL (TOP AND BOTTOM)

There are two other places where you can get feedback from the abdominal wall during active expiration: the xyphoid process (the point just underneath your breastbone and where the ribs start to part), and the point just above your pubic arch.

1. Press with your fingers on both these areas. They represent the top and bottom of the abdominis rectus muscle in the abdominal wall (commonly called the 'six pack' in bodybuilders).

2. Roll an 'R' vigorously. If you can't roll an 'R', use the lip-trill instead. As the abdominis muscle contracts, you will feel it pushing out under your fingers. (You are still sending the area just below your navel towards your backbone to create airflow.)

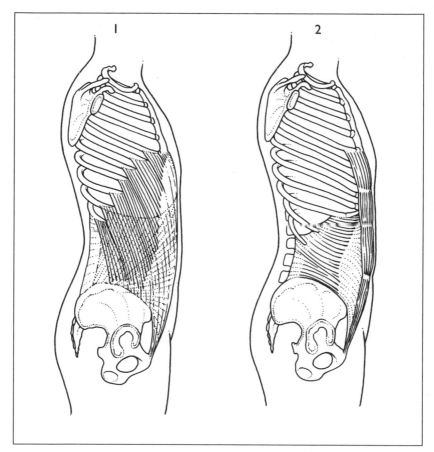

The muscles of the abdominal wall: diagram 1 – the internal and external obliques; diagram 2 – transverse abdominis and rectus abdominis

3. Roll an 'R' or lip-trill up and down through your range; don't sing, just vocalise. Notice the feedback you get from these two points as you are vocalising.

Awareness exercise 3: THE DIAMOND

The title of this exercise refers to the shape of the four points for the supporting muscles of the abdominal wall. Each of the points represents a place where muscles join on.

1. In the previous two exercises we worked with the two sides of the waistband, the xyphoid process and the point just above the pubic arch. Put all four points together; you will need to alternate between them as you only have two hands.

2. Repeat the rolled 'R' or lip-
   blowing sequence moving up and
   down through your range.

Notice what happens. You need to
work the four corners of the
diamond while keeping the centre of
the diamond flexible.

How does it work? Intra-abdominal pressure

The abdominal wall is a long way
from the vocal folds. It may be difficult to visualise how work in the
abdominal wall can help to maintain
or create sub-glottic pressure. Your
body has a number of pressure
systems; intra-abdominal pressure is
one of them.

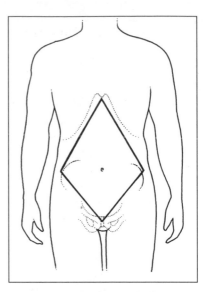

Diagram 3: The diamond of support, after Chapman

1. People often use a balloon as an image for the lungs. I want you to
visualise two balloons: one representing the chest (upper) cavity, and one
representing the abdominal (lower) cavity.

   2. The abdominal cavity is sealed and separated from the chest cavity
by the diaphragm. Because the diaphragm is flexible, it is possible to
create pressure in the abdominal cavity and push the diaphragm upward
into the chest cavity.

   3. The chest cavity is not sealed. It has the valve of the vocal folds at the
top end. The vibrating vocal folds can create 'back pressure' against the
pressure sent up from the abdominal cavity, which in turn creates
pressure in the chest. This back-pressure is the sub-glottic pressure that
we need for singing.

The muscles you are using when you work the 'diamond' to create intra-
abdominal pressure are the external and internal oblique muscles and the
transversus abdominis. All three muscles are paired (there is a set each
side of the body), and are broad and flat in shape, attaching to the ribcage
and parts of the pelvic crest. The transversus abdominis and internal
obliques (the deeper layers) also link via tendons and connective tissue to
the spinal column and so form a tube around the body.

   These three sets of muscles, together with rectus abdominis at the
front, form a strong sheath for your abdominal contents.

Posture and the diamond of support

The muscles of the abdominal wall are active in stabilising posture. We use them for standing, sitting up, and for forward and sideways bends. The body is set up to work efficiently for many different tasks, and your posture will vary according to the task in hand. In this instance if your standing posture is poor, the use of your abdominal wall is likely to be poor too. If you do not have a good sense of where these support muscles are, it would be a good idea to an exercise class or to the gym, and to ask the instructor to devise a programme for you. Exercises that put you in touch with these muscles – lateral bends, twists and curl-ups – will be helpful for your use of support. The Pilates system is very good for actors and concentrates on strength and flexibilty in the core abdominal region. There are a number of classes available with trained instructors who understand the needs of the profession. Here are some general guidelines towards an efficient standing posture;

1. Stand with your feet comfortably apart (for most people this is at hip width) so that you have a solid base.

2. The knees should not be locked; locked knees put the whole spine out of balance and might cause you difficulties with the recoil breath.

3. Pay attention to the tilt of your pelvis; if you are over-arching your back and tipping the pelvis backwards, you will not get full movement from the diaphragm when you breathe in. Conversely do not slump the body by tipping the pelvis forwards; you cannot engage the muscles of the abdominal wall if you are slumped.

4. Keeping the head over the shoulders, feel that your spine is in alignment. Don't try to straighten the spine, but be aware of its full length.

5. The shoulders need to be relaxed, with the arms hanging easily.

6. Avoid collapsing the rectus abdominis along the front of the body, particularly just below the sternum. Organise the front of your body so that you can utilise the top and bottom of your 'diamond' efficiently.

The following exercise is useful for more sustained singing tasks such as singing classic book ballads.

Exercise 3: WORKING TO SUSTAIN

1. Sing this five note scale to a rolled 'R' or to a lip-trill. Go up and down the scale in one breath.

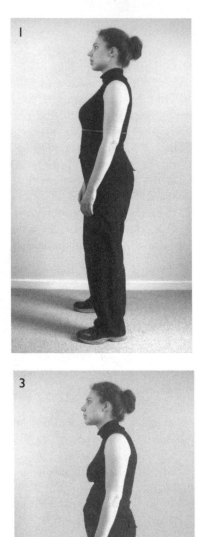

1 *Balanced posture*

2 *Over-arched posture*

3 *Slumped posture*

2. Repeat the scale, this time starting a semitone (half-tone) higher. Continue this sequence, allowing time to recoil in between each scale. Put in as many beats as you need at first to allow yourself time to recoil; you can always reduce the number and length of the beats in between as you become more experienced.

3. Extend the scale to this nine note scale given.

You'll find that the exercise above takes a little more concentration on your waistband muscles. Surprisingly, you may find that you are not taking in any more air than you did for the five-note scale; if this is the case, it is because you are beginning to use your breath more efficiently. Some students are so fixated on breathing in that they never allow themselves to find the point when they run out of breath. It really is OK to feel that you are running out of breath.

Food for thought

Below are some further exercises for awareness in breath use. They are designed to help you think about breath management in a flexible way, so that it does not become divorced from the act of singing text.

Awareness exercise 4: REVIEWING ONSET OF TONE

Review the work we did in Chapter 2, (pages 15–16) to control onset of tone. Repeat each onset several times until you become aware of what is happening with your breath.
1. What happens when you do the glottal onset? The breath stops before you make the sound. What stops the breath, the abdomen, or the vocal folds? Find out what needs to happen to allow the breath to come through after closing the folds.

2. Do the aspirate onset. This time, the sound is made on the breath. Find out what needs to happen to stop and start the sound using this onset.
3. Do the simultaneous onset. Notice that you need to hold the breath with the vocal folds open as a preparation for this onset. Find out what needs to happen to hold the breath when the vocal folds are open.

With each onset, because you were doing something different with the vocal folds, you managed your breath differently. These changes at vocal folds level are an important part of creating voice quality.

Awareness exercise 5: CONSONANTS

1. Articulate the following voiceless fricatives: 'f', 'sh' /ʃ/, 's'. Notice what is happening with the breath; they require a lot of air in their production.
2. Sing syllables beginning with the voiceless fricatives, putting a vowel after each one. What do you notice? You cannot start voicing until after you have articulated the fricative, and the fricative uses up a lot of air. In fact, you probably needed to breathe after each sound.
3. Repeat stages 1 and 2 with these stopped consonants: 't', 'p', 'k'. Monitor your breath use. Again you will observe that you cannot start voicing until after you have made the consonant, and that, in the case of these sounds, the breath is stopped before you make them. A burst of air follows the consonant, which also disturbs the sensation of breath 'flow'.

Song assignment: YOUR SONG

Pick a simple song to work on that you already know.
1. Sing the melody through, using either the rolled 'R', or lip-trill, or voiced fricatives 'v', 'z' or 'ge' /ʒ/.
2. As you sing, monitor your abdominal wall. Check that you can recoil when you need to breathe in. Check the diamond of support when you are singing.
3. Repeat the song, this time using the words. Monitor your abdominal wall as before.
4. Sing the song again. Notice when the breath seems to stop, when the airflow is increased, and if you are using different types of onset.

What conclusions can you draw from the last two awareness exercises and the song assignment? The main conclusion is simply that our breath use cannot feel the same all the time. What is required for efficient breath use in singing is a flexible and muscular breathing apparatus that will allow the breath to work appropriately according to the vocal task.

When I was training as a singer, it sometimes felt as though I was on a quest for the holy grail of 'the breath'. I realise now that there is no perfect breathing system, only a body of knowledge that performers and teachers have found to work in practice. Most of the breath work I do with clients is remedial; fixing bad habits and getting rid of inappropriate effort. If you are having difficulties with your breathing, start by analysing the source of the problem. Use this checklist:

1. Am I allowing the breath to drop in? (If not, work on the elastic recoil.)

2. Am I impeding the breath by constricting in the larynx? Notice if your in-breath is noisy or if you close up suddenly inside the larynx at the ends of phrases. (To remedy these, practise the recoil and the sustaining exercises, monitoring constriction via the silent laugh.)

3. Do I have sufficient airflow? (If not, work the voiced fricatives, rolled 'R' or lip-trill exercises.)

4. Am I over-breathing, that is either taking in or pushing out too much air for the singing task? (If you are, monitor your airflow and examine your onset of tone.)

Work your muscles, and do not make the task of breathing too complicated. If your body is in balance, if you are free from laryngeal constriction and if your vocal folds are working efficiently, your breath use will sort itself out.

Training your Voice

The information in Chapters 5–9 deal with important aspects of vocal training that preoccupy most singers and singing teachers: managing tension, working the range, finding resonance, dealing with gear changes, vowel placement and dynamic control. These are essential skills for the trained performer, and you may need to invest some time in mastering them. Keen amateur singers and other professional voice users can also benefit from working these exercises. Most of the exercises given are musically simple as I find this preferable to complicated scales and arpeggios. I feel it is important to get the instrument in good working order before asking it to perform musically complex manoeuvres. These can always be built in later. Exercises that are song-based work just as well in many instances.

Some of these exercises will become favourites in your vocal warm-up. In the text I have suggested which ones might be a regular requirement. A healthy voice does not need a long warm-up. Something between 10 and 20 minutes is usually sufficient. Mental and physical preparation (making sure you are alert and ready to work) are just as important to the vocal performer as the actual warm-up. I recommend you allow for these factors when preparing for auditions and performances.

General British Vowel Key

Note: When a single letter 'r' is a part of a vowel Respelling, it is not pronounced.

Lexical set in SMALL CAPS and indications of the vowel locations in **bold**.

Phonetics	'Respelling'	Representative Words
/ɑː/	'AH'	PALM, BATH, m**ar**k
/ɜː/	'ER'	NURSE, b**ir**d, conf**er**
/ɔː/	'AW'	THOUGHT, w**al**ker, l**aw**
/iː/	'EE'	FLEECE, m**ea**n, f**ee**
/uː/	'OO'	GOOSE, cr**u**de, b**oo**ts
/ɪ/	'ih'	KIT, st**i**ll, w**i**cked
/æ/	'ae'	TRAP, b**a**nned, spl**a**shed
/e/	'eh'	DRESS, t**e**nth, s**e**ction
/ʌ/	'UH'	STRUT , w**o**rried, w**o**nders
/ɒ/	'aw'	LOT, s**o**ft, c**o**stly
/ʊ/	'ou'	FOOT, c**ou**ld, p**u**t
/ə/	'uh'	COMMA, LETTER, tak**e**n, **a**lone
/ɪə/	'ir'	NEAR, w**ei**rd, r**ear**
/eə/	'air'	SQUARE, d**are**, f**air**
/ʊə/	'oor'	CURE, p**oor**, l**ure**
/eɪ/	'ey'	FACE, s**ay**, aw**ay**
/aɪ/	'ay'	PRICE, t**i**me, compl**y**
/ɔɪ/	'oy'	CHOICE, andr**oi**d, pl**oy**
/əʊ/	'oh'	GOAT, s**ew**, ag**o**
/aʊ/	'ow'	MOUTH, l**ou**d, v**ow**
/eɪə/	'eyor'	pl**ayer**, conv**eyor**, sl**ayer**
/aɪə/	'ire'	sc**ie**nce, v**io**let, f**ire**
/ɔɪə/	'oyer'	l**awyer**, r**oyal**, t**oil**
/əʊə/	'oer'	l**ower**, m**ower**, bl**ower**
/aʊə/	'ower'	p**ower**, s**our**, fl**ower**

General American Vowel Key

Note: When a single letter 'rr' is a part of a vowel Respelling, it is pronounced.

Lexical set in SMALL CAPS and indications of the vowel locations in **bold**.

Phonetics	'Respelling'	Representative Words
/ɑː/	'AH'	PALM, s**o**vereign, marath**o**n
/ɝː/	'URR'	NURSE, pref**er**, ref**er**
/ɔː/	'aww'	THOUGHT, wr**o**ng, s**aw**
/iː/	'EE'	FLEECE, m**ea**n, f**ee**
/uː/	'OO'	GOOSE, cr**u**de, b**oo**ts
/ɪ/	'ih'	KIT, st**i**ll, wick**e**d
/æ/	'ae'	TRAP, BATH, spl**a**shed
/ɛ/	'eh'	DRESS, t**e**nth, s**e**ction
/ʌ/	'UH'	STRUT, w**a**s, wh**a**t, **u**nder
/ʊ/	'ou'	FOOT, c**ou**ld, p**u**t
/ə/	'uh'	COMMA, th**e**, **a**lone, tak**e**n
/ɚ/	'urr'	LETTER, int**er**national, sug**ar**
/ɪɚ/	'irr'	NEAR, w**eir**d, app**ear**
/ɛɚ/	'err'	SQUARE, d**are**, f**air**
/ɑɚ/	'arr'	START, s**ar**dine, t**ar**
/ɔɚ/	'orr'	FORCE, **Or**pheus, p**ore**
/ʊɚ/	'oorr'	CURE, end**ure**, cont**our**
/eɪ/	'ey'	FACE, s**ay**, aw**ay**
/aɪ/	'ay'	PRICE, t**i**me, compl**y**
/ɔɪ/	'oy'	CHOICE, andr**oi**d, pl**oy**
/oʊ/	'oh'	GOAT, v**o**gue, fell**ow**
/aʊ/	'ow'	MOUTH, l**ou**d, v**ow**
/eɪɚ/	'eyurr'	pl**aye**r, conv**eyo**r, sl**aye**r
/aɪɚ/	'ayurr'	d**ire**, adm**ire**, f**ire**
/ɔɪɚ/	'oyurr'	l**awye**r, r**oya**l, t**oil**
/oʊɚ/	'ohurr'	l**owe**r, m**owe**r, bl**owe**r
/aʊɚ/	'owurr'	p**owe**r, s**our**, fl**owe**r

General English Consonant Key

Note: consonant examples indicated in **bold**.

Phonetics	'Respelling'	Representative Words
/p/	'p'	**p**eel, a**pp**roach, stoo**p**
/b/	'b'	**b**ell, tri**b**ute, tu**b**e
/m/	'm'	**m**arry, ca**m**paign, handso**m**e
/f/	'f'	**f**ellow, a**f**ter, stu**ff**
/v/	'v'	**v**ery, a**v**erage, gi**v**e
/w/	'w'	**w**estern, stal**w**art, a**w**ay
/θ/	'th'	**th**ink, a**th**lete, tru**th**
/ð/	'~~th~~'	**th**is, ra**th**er, bli**th**e
/t/	't'	**t**ime, fu**t**ile, ha**t**
/d/	'd'	**d**eep, a**dd**ition, be**d**
/s/	's'	**s**ip, a**ss**ume, bli**ss**
/z/	'z'	**z**est, pre**s**ume, head**s**
/l/	'l'	**l**ast, simi**l**ar, pu**ll**
/n/	'n'	**n**either, a**n**tique, fu**n**
/ʃ/	'sh'	**sh**ift, vi**c**ious, po**sh**
/ʒ/	'ge'	mea**s**ure, fu**s**ion, vi**s**ion
/tʃ/	'ch'	**ch**est, a**ch**ieve, lur**ch**
/dʒ/	'j'	**j**ump, a**dj**acent, ba**dge**
/r/	'r'	**r**ed, a**rr**ow, **r**u**r**al
/j/	'y'	**y**esterday, can**y**on, vine**y**ard
/k/	'k'	**k**ept, sil**k**en, sha**ck**
/g/	'g'	**g**uest, be**g**otten, bi**g**
/ŋ/	'ng'	si**ng**, li**n**k, Li**n**coln
/h/	'h'	**h**ave, a**h**ead, **h**uge

Chapter 5

Developing the three octave siren

Though the chapter title reads like a challenge, it is not an impossible one. Many of my clients develop a two-and-a-half to three-octave range in their siren. You, too, can achieve this using the correct approach. The siren is an incredibly versatile vocal exercise, useful for a quick vocal warm-up, for developing range and targeting gear changes, for improving your sense of pitch, and for programming song melodies into the muscle memory. Dealing with tension and developing vocal range are two of the major issues in singing training. The exercises that follow will enable you to target these topics at the best time in your training – early on.

MONITORING CONSTRICTION DURING TRAINING

Negative practice can be useful in helping to develop awareness. In Chapter 2 we explored two opposite sensations in the larynx: constriction and retraction. In the following two exercises you will become aware of the sound of constriction, the feel of it (from both inside and outside the larynx), and the image of space inside the larynx. The aim of these exercises is to separate the action of the true and false folds; this will happen when you find the sensation of a silent laugh. There are three positions to explore: neutral (relaxed), constricted and retracted.

Exercise 1: THE THREE POSITIONS OF THE FALSE VOCAL FOLDS

Use your thumbs to create an image of the false vocal folds:

Thumbs slightly apart = neutral　　*Thumbs together = constriction*　　*Thumbs wide apart = retraction*

1. Breathe out through your mouth on a gentle sigh. Only use breath for this, no voice.
   Be aware of the sensation (relaxed) and the sound (light and breathy). Visualise the air passing through your larynx, using the image of air passing through a hollow tube. This is the neutral position.
2. Breathe out again, forming an 'EE' /iː/ without sound. Aim to tighten up in the larynx as you breathe out. Focus your attention on the inside of your larynx.
   i. The sound will be like a forced whisper (think of Marlon Brando in *The Godfather*);
   ii. The image will be that the tube of your larynx has narrowed;
   iii. The feel is tight and restricted inside your larynx; outside you can feel the abdominal muscles working to push the breath out.
   You might like to use your thumbs to visualise the space inside your larynx closing up, using light to medium effort. This is the constricted position

There are many places that you can constrict in the vocal tract. For example, unvoiced fricatives require a type of constriction to create noise with the breath. This is not what we are looking for here. Avoid making the sound of constriction in your mouth using the tongue or the soft palate. Focus further down in the vocal tract and inside the larynx.

3. Repeat stages 1 and 2, and then suddenly laugh silently using the impulse of a giggle or chuckle. Now focus on what was different:
   i. The sound will have changed: during the constriction, there was noise (turbulence), but when you laughed silently the noise went away;
   ii. The image will be that the tube of your larynx has widened;
   iii. There will be a sense of width inside your larynx, possibly of something having moved apart or away. Outside, your abdominal wall will stop pushing and may start moving with the laughter.
   You might like to spread your thumbs wide apart to represent the space inside the larynx. This is the retracted position.

Repeat stages 1–3, then:
4. Continue breathing out as you hold the retracted position. You may find that, as soon as you have reached it, the air rushes out all at once. This is because there is nothing stopping it. You can attend to this by controlling the release of air from the abdominal wall if you like, but it really doesn't matter at this stage. The important thing is to hold the laugh posture while being able to breathe in or out.
5. Notice that holding the laugh posture requires effort. The sensation is not the same as for the 'neutral' posture in stage 1. At this point you

will find it useful to give the sensation a score in effort level. Use a scale of 1–10, where 1 is the least effort and 10 the most. What is your personal effort level required in finding the retracted posture in the larynx? Make a mental note of the number as it will be useful for embedding muscle memory in the future.

6. Repeat stages 1–5, and then sing a note.

Exercise 2: EXTERNAL MONITORING

You may need to refer back to 'laryngeal orienteering' in Chapter 3 to help with your monitoring. A clear difference can be felt between a relaxed posture and a retracted one, though it is not as dramatic as the difference between constricted and retracted. Use the photograph on page 45 as a further guide.

1 Work through Exercise 1 again. Very gently, using a thumb and finger or two fingers, monitor the two sides of the thyroid cartilage as you go through each stage.

2. Make a note of the differences you feel underneath your fingers.

i. It is common to feel the larynx push up and in, as if it tightened up from the inside.

ii. When you find the retracted position for the false vocal folds, you may feel the sides of the thyroid widen as if opening out.

iii. Alternatively, you might feel as though your larynx simply 'softens' whereas before it felt 'hard'.

iv. Repeat stages 1–5 from Exercise 1, and then sing a note.

It is normal for people to experience these changes in the larynx differently. Find the monitoring device that works most reliably for you. Some people find it helpful to use an elastic band wound around the thumbs (clasp your hands together first) to help them feel and visualise the difference between relaxed and retracted false vocal folds.

Further monitoring:

i. Notice the effort required in maintaining the laugh posture – without sound, with sound, and in various parts of your range.

ii. Notice changes in your general body posture as you do the exercises. Aim to isolate the sense of constriction and retraction solely in the larynx by gradually relaxing other efforts such as:

    a. smiling or grinning;

    b. pumping the abdominal wall (something we normally do when we laugh);

    c. tensing the tongue;

    d. tensing the jaw;

    e. moving the shoulders up and down.

Finally, you may be aware of a difference in breath use when singing with retraction. This can happen because you have opened the space wider in the larynx, and the vocal folds are able to vibrate more freely. Enjoy the greater sense of vocal freedom that you experience as a result of mastering retraction!

Training is about awareness and working muscles. Ideally, having trained and rehearsed, you can forget about technical functions and focus on performing. As a working actor you will want to maintain good vocal health. Therefore, you need to have an awareness of changes in your own vocal and

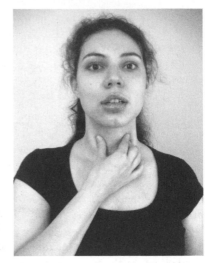

Monitoring retraction

physical effort levels that might lead to laryngeal constriction: in training, in rehearsal, and in performance situations that require emotions *in extremis.*

DEVELOPING YOUR RANGE

In Chapter 1, Exercise 4, we explored sirening as an exercise in awareness for effort levels and vocal range. Here is some more detailed work that you can do with the siren towards achieving your goal of a three-octave range.

Exercise 3: RANDOM SIRENING

1. Using the effort number that you established for retraction in Exercise 1, stage 5, ensure that you are already retracted as you make a small whining sound on an 'ng' /ŋ/ (as in the word 'sing').
2. Start to move the siren around a little, moving up and down in pitch like this:

Notice that you need hardly any breath to make this sound and that, if you are in a comfortable part of your range, it takes very little effort. The sound needs to be small and quiet as this is a 'feel' exercise. It is fine to stop and start the exercise at any point provided you retain your silent laugh posture. Breathe if you need to, but less is more in this exercise.

3. Move your siren further up and down in pitch. Then go up and down as far as you can, observing or feeling for any significant changes as you do so. You can either look in the mirror or place your fingers gently on your larynx as we did in Chapter 3.

Observe or feel that:

i. the larynx tends to move up and down with the pitch;

ii. the tongue tends to push up against the soft palate, more so as you go higher;

iii. there is a sense of muscular effort around the sides and back of the neck, and this may increase at certain points in your range;

iv. things seem to get smaller at the back of your mouth as you go up in pitch.

4. Repeat stages 1–3, monitoring retraction, the volume of the siren and your breath use.

5. Monitor your body for extraneous tensions. Continue to siren as you:

i. chew with the front to soften jaw tension. Notice if you want to open your jaw wide as this is a sign of jaw tension. Keep it flexible;

ii. drop your shoulders, lengthen the neck and elongate the whole spine;

iii. walk around the room so that you do not have unnecessary body tension.

You are now isolating specific muscle functions. Monitor your personal effort levels using the work from Chapter 2, Awareness exercise 4. Use the *Isolation Checklist* on page 14 whenever you are working new topics in the book from now on.

If your voice cracks when you siren, it's OK; it just means you are normal. Your voice, like any other pipe, is an imperfect instrument. There are numerous factors that contribute to the changes of voice quality that are usually referred to as changes of registration, and we will explore these later. At this point focus solely on the two mechanical changes that will help you complete your siren.

Exercise 4: TARGETING YOUR BREAKS

The aim of this exercise is to find out where your voice wants to change gear by allowing it to crack, break or change quality. You will find that there are two significant change points:

1. Go up (or down) to the point where your siren feels or sounds unstable or even cuts out on you. Make a note of where this is in your range. It may be about a third of the way through your range (women) or roughly two-thirds of the way (men).
2. Practise doing the siren too loudly so that you can emphasise the changes. What happens when you do this? Women tend to experience a noticeable change in voice quality around a third of the way up through their range; men tend to experience a noticeable change in voice quality two thirds of the way up through their range.
3. Continue on up through your range with the siren. Do you have a second gear change? It may feel as though you have hit a ceiling in your siren or that your siren cuts out for a moment and then continues on further up. Make a note of where this second gear change occurs and any sensations that go with it.

Most voices find it difficult to reach the top of the range unless they allow this second gear change to take place.

Smoothing out the gear changes

There are several issues here:

1. *Constriction.* You will need to monitor constriction during gear changes. Look out for roughness in your sound, tightness in sensation, or your voice stopping altogether.

2. *Volume.* You are more likely to run into difficulties if you do the siren loudly, as this requires more breath pressure and increased work in the vocal folds.

3. *Effort levels.* Avoid pushing with the breath to negotiate either gear change. It is not the breath doing the work here.

4. *Effort levels.* Support your larynx in making these changes by working muscles outside the larynx in the vocal tract.

5. *Changes in vocal fold mass.* For the first gear change you will need to assist the vocal folds in thinning and lengthening.

6. *Changes in height of the larynx.* For the second gear change you will need to allow the larynx to rise.

Monitoring devices:

i. In monitoring constriction, use 'thumbs apart' to help visualise the space inside the larynx; alternatively you could use an elastic band wound around your thumbs. Stretch the elastic band as you think of the silent laugh.

ii. Practise breathing out before doing your siren. This will put you in touch with how little breath you need to make it.

iii. Listen out for unnecessary changes in volume. Keep your sound levels small.

iv. Support your larynx by engaging muscles at the back and sides of the neck. Put your hand on the back of your neck at the base of the skull, where there is a slight depression (the occipital groove). Push up and back with the base of your skull into your hand. This will have the effect of straightening the cervical spine. You need to maintain this posture for a few notes only, and then you should be able to continue with no trouble. Alternatively you could place the palm of your hand on the crown of your head. Push down with the palm, then up with the head into the palm. This will have the same effect as the previous device.

v. Tilt the thyroid cartilage. Muscles that tilt the thyroid enable you to reset the length and tensioning of your vocal fold muscles. Use the sensation of 'tilting' from Chapter 3 (page 23) and the sound of the whimpering puppy or whining child to help you 'thin' your vocal folds as you go up in pitch towards the first gear change. Be aware of releasing the tilt slowly as you come down through the gear change. Like a good driver using manual gear changes, you need to plan ahead.

vi. Monitor raising the larynx for the second gear change, placing your fingers on the larynx, as we did in Chapter 3 (page 18). Notice if your desire is to push down with the larynx and tongue as you go to the top of your siren. Keep the tongue high in the mouth by thinking 'EEng' /iːŋ/ rather than 'UHng' /ʌŋ/. There is a subtle difference in sound quality when you make this change. Visualise your larynx being pulled upwards, like an old-fashioned lift in a lift shaft.

If you are thinking that this all appears rather complex, let me reassure you: it doesn't get any harder than this! The negotiation of gear changes in the voice has preoccupied singing teachers for centuries, and many students agonise over how to do it. If you follow the instructions above, you will be able to do a full siren without any audible changes in quality and without cracks and breaks. You may well still feel the gear changes, but they will be smoothed out and less obvious from the outside.

Gear changes and the vocal registers

A variety of terms are used by singers and singing teachers to describe the changes you have just been exploring in your range. Some of them are quite confusing, and singing teachers still argue about them. In Chapter 1 we explored some ideas about head and chest 'register'. This terminology refers to changes of voice quality that happen in a certain part of your vocal range. Voice quality could be described as vocal colour or timbre. Because singers sustain pitch across a broad range of notes, they are usually very aware of these changes in quality. In traditional 'bel canto' training the aim has been to minimise these changes in quality, hence the many exercises to blend or mix the vocal registers. In musical theatre work, this blending is not so important. What you need to learn is how to negotiate the two main mechanical changes in your voice as you go through your range. You will find this helpful whatever voice quality you are making. Later in the book we shall be learning how to create different voice qualities by choice.

Application in music and song

So far you have been working the siren as a noise. Sirening on specific pitches is just the same. Sirening in octaves is a good way to practise pitch leaps, and it helps to develop vocal agility. The extent of your siren will depend on the boundaries of your range; no voice is the same as another. You may be surprised to find that your siren now covers two-and-a-half to three octaves. If you are unsure about your range, work through the following exercise with a vocal coach or friend who plays keyboard, and 'chart' your range, including the change points. If you don't read music it doesn't matter; working the siren will improve your feel for pitch so that you will begin to know where you are in your voice even without accompaniment.

Exercise 5: OCTAVE SIRENS

1. Using the same amount of effort as before, siren up an octave from a low note and back again.

ng_____

2. Keep the silent laugh posture after you've finished the leap and take a small breath in.
3. Move up a step and repeat.
4. Continue on up, step by step until you reach the top of your range.

ng_____   ng_____   ng_____

5. Keeping the octave leap, work your way down again, step by step.
   The siren often goes awry when the student starts to sing it. Remember that it is exactly the same process as before, and:

i. avoid pushing air;
ii. keep your tongue and palate together at all times, even for the high notes;
iii. siren softly, gliding between pairs of notes so that there are no gaps (essentially you are singing all the pitches in-between the two notes, but very fast);
iv. notice where you feel your soft palate wanting to lift and the larynx rising; at this point push up with your tongue and palate together;
v. push backwards a little with the base of the skull and lengthen the cervical spine as you negotiate any change points.

Moving from sircning to vowels

During the four previous exercises you have been working on 'ng' /ŋ/ with the back of the tongue touching the soft palate all the time. We are now going to take the siren a stage further in application, moving from 'ng' to vowels.

Look at the musical example below, which illustrates stages 1 and 2 for Exercise 6.

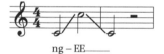

ng – EE⎯⎯

You will see that in stage 2 you are going to change from 'ng' /ŋ/ to 'EE', once you have hit the top note. This requires you to move your soft palate away from the back of the tongue. If you are unsure about this, look back at Chapter 1, page 7, where you learned how to locate the soft palate. There are more advanced exercises for the palate in Chapter 6.

Exercise 6: FROM SIREN TO VOWEL

This is a variation of Exercise 5.
1. Using the same notes as before, glide up the octave on 'ng' /ŋ/. Sing the top note for a little longer as you move from 'ng' /ŋ/ to 'EE'.
2. Come down again still singing 'EE', keeping everything else the same as for the siren: the silent laugh, the neck lengthening, volume of breath and so on. The only thing you have changed is the position of the soft palate. The sound will still be quiet, but it should be clear and sound 'easy'.
3. You can do this exercise with other vowels as well, but always start with 'EE'.

Exercises 3 to 6 are excellent basic vocal exercises. They each warm up your voice, target your gear changes, and get you thinking about pitch. When you do these exercises, rather like a ballerina at the bar, you are warming up the small muscles of your voice. Exercise 3 has an additional advantage in that it can be done anywhere and does not disturb the neighbours.

Trouble with pitching

I don't hold with the term tone-deaf: 99% of people who do not sing in tune can hear melodies, but they just have difficulty in reproducing them. Those who have genuine difficulties with pitching often absorb negative ideas about their voice, because they have been told to mouth in the choir at school, or have been laughed at by friends and family. I have found that dealing with laryngeal constriction – enabling the vocal folds to vibrate properly – goes a long way towards solving pitch problems. It is interesting that when someone has a difficulty with pitch, we try to teach him or her to sing in tune by either singing scales or bashing out single notes on the piano (the 'can't you hear that?' technique). People with pitching problems usually have difficulty making the link between what they are feeling in the vocal tract and what they are hearing. Pitch needs to be felt as well as heard.

Feeling the pitch

1. Get in touch with the vocal mechanism so that you can rely on kinaesthetic feedback, as well as auditory feedback. Work with retraction, and simply sing your own notes.
2. Work the siren: it helps you to map out the feeling of up and down. It also builds into your muscle memory how hard you need to work in certain parts of your range.
3. Siren without trying to make notes at all at first; just make the noise. Then work with big intervals. (Note that it is not desirable for novice singers to start with the fine-tuning. We do not ask children when they are learning to write to begin with calligraphy; we allow them to make big movements!)
4. Avoid working with the piano. The piano is tuned according to what is known as equal temperament, which makes it difficult for the human ear to differentiate easily between one interval and another. When you are learning to pitch, get your teacher or vocal coach to sing the notes for you, preferably at pitch in your octave.
5. Work the siren on vowels as well as 'ng' /ŋ/, working from the octave to smaller intervals of a 5th to a 3rd and so on. Gradually you will begin to trust the connection between your voice and your ear.

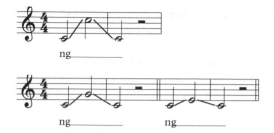

ng

ng   ng

6. Work with Exercises 1, 2, 3, and 5 in Chapter 6 for the soft palate and control of the nasal port. You will begin to feel that you can organise the different sensations you have in your instrument, and will build in reliable muscular feedback. The soft palate exercises are very physical and will give you something to pin the notes on.

7. Move on to the anchoring exercises in Chapter 7 (Exercises 1–3). Many people are singing the right pitch but sound out of tune because the note isn't resonating properly. I have found this particularly with singers who have big voices. A big voice in the early stages of training will often be somewhat wild in its pitching. Using an analogy, how would you do in your first driving lesson if someone put you behind the wheel of a Porsche or a Daimler? Anchoring will help you to resonate better and give you control over the size of your voice.

So that's it. Now you have the full keyboard for your instrument. Whether or not it is three octaves, remember that if you can siren it you can sing it.

Song assignment: YOUR SONG

Find a song – almost any song will do. Choose one that you do not know very well yet, but for which you have either the sheet music or a reliable recording.

1. Listen to the melody or play it on a keyboard.
2. Phrase by phrase, or with any small unit of the melodic line, siren your way through the song. Make sure that you siren seamlessly between pitches that belong together in the same phrase. Inexperienced singers will often try to hit each note with the vocal folds in order to check their tuning. Remember that the voice is not a percussion instrument. If two notes belong together in one phrase and there is no rest, there is no need for the vocal folds to stop vibrating before pitching the next note. The pitching mechanism is in the larynx: if you are set up correctly, your vocal folds will soon make the minute adjustments required to change pitch without much prompting from you.
3. Breathe with the sense of the words wherever possible, and put in the rests where they are written (or indicated on the recording). When you are learning a new song, it doesn't matter how many times you need to

breathe; just do what is comfortable to begin with. As your muscles begin to learn the shape of the melody, you will find that the breathing becomes easier.

4. Check that you are retracted all the time. A good way to do this is to sing the song silently, mouthing the words as you go, and breathing out as if you were singing. This way you can concentrate on maintaining the laugh posture and listen with the muscles. It also gives you the opportunity to observe what is going on in the abdominal wall – are you allowing the abdominal wall to release as you recoil into each new breath?

5. Siren the song again.

6. Repeat the song with the words; you are already programming the song into your muscular memory. This is part of a process that we shall use later in the book when we look at how to learn new material quickly.

7. Make a note of any corners that you find difficult in the song. Are you constricting on these notes? Are they at change points in your range? You can solve these problems with the techniques you have learned in this chapter.

Chapter 6

The nasal port

A resonant voice is something that most performers and trainers seek. The soft palate has a key role in controlling nasal and oral resonance. To this end many training exercises for improving resonance will work the soft palate in a general way. The soft palate will also be worked during consonant routines that involve moving from nasal and velar consonants into vowels. Specific work on the muscle groups that move the soft palate are rarely given, and there is confusion as to how the soft palate itself moves during some common exercise routines. Students may be told they have a 'lazy' or 'tense' soft palate, but be unclear about how to address these. This is such an important subject that I have devoted a whole chapter to this structure.

WHAT IS THE NASAL PORT?

Look at Diagram 1: the sagittal section of the vocal tract.

If you look at the hard palate, which forms the roof of the mouth, you will see that it extends into a non-bony area (the shaded areas indicate bone in the diagram) and ends in the uvula. You can feel this if you run your tongue backwards along the roof of the mouth until you reach the soft, fleshy area and the dangling uvula. Now look at Diagrams 2–4, which show how the soft palate can be moved. Notice that it may either:

1. seal off the oral (mouth) cavity by moving down to the tongue, *allowing sound into the nose* (Diagram 2), or,

2. seal off the nasal cavity by pulling up and back onto the back wall of the pharynx, *stopping sound from going into the nose* (Diagram 4), or,

3. be relaxed, hanging downwards, therefore *not sealing either cavity* from the other (Diagram 3).

This 'sealing' action is why we talk about the nasal port: it is a doorway between the mouth and the nose. When your nasal port is fully open the palate is down and the sound will be nasal; when your nasal port is fully closed the palate is up and the sound will be oral. When the nasal port is half-open (or half-closed) you will produce vowels that are *nasalised* and your tonal quality will be defined as 'nasal'.

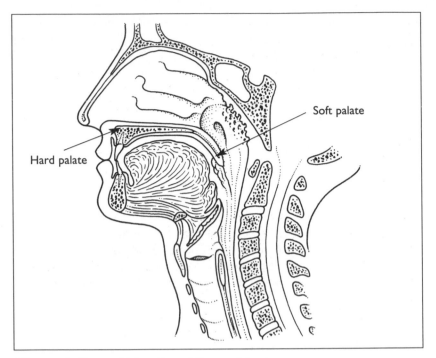

Diagram 1: The sagittal section of the vocal tract

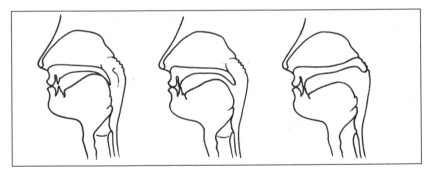

Diagrams 2–4: Positions of the palate

These actions are part of the 'primary functioning' of the voice that I spoke about in Chapter 2. We need to close the nasal port to stop food going up into the nose in swallowing, and we need to open the nasal port to take air in through the nose.

The soft palate is actually a complex group of muscles. It can be tensed, raised, depressed or relaxed. It is pulled upwards and backwards by the levator palatini muscles and tensed by the tensor palatini muscles. It is pulled downwards by the palatoglossal muscles, which attach into the back of the tongue (glossus). While you cannot necessarily feel independent movement of these muscles, you will certainly feel the effects of them working, and therefore you can monitor the action of your soft palate. Much of this activity takes place above the roof of the mouth.

For this reason, it is important not to collapse the cervical spine if you want your palate to work efficiently. People with poor head and neck posture often have difficulty controlling their nasal port.

Here are a few common *misconceptions* about the nasal port:

1. The soft palate is always up when you are singing.

2. The soft palate lifts automatically when you breathe in.

3. You have no independent control over the soft palate.

4. You will get a brighter tone if you sing into your nose.

5. The contemporary musical theatre sound is nasal.

Independent control of the soft palate can be surprisingly difficult. Here are some exercises in awareness that will prepare you for work on the soft palate.

Awareness exercise 1: FINDING THE SEAL

This exercise will enable you to feel where the soft palate is located and how it acts as a doorway between the nose and the mouth.

1. Make a 'p' with your lips. Practise it a couple of times, and then hold the build-up to the 'p' without releasing your lips. Note that there is a build-up of breath behind the closed lips.
2. Still holding your breath behind the 'p', attempt to breathe out through your nose.
3. Notice what happens when you do this, trying it out several times, experimenting with harder and softer 'pushes' with the breath.

To begin with, you are probably just aware of a pressure suddenly being released, and of the breath coming out of your nose. With subsequent repetitions, focus on the feeling at the back of your nose. Notice that something has to move to let the breath out into the nose. That is your soft palate, moving from a raised (closed port) position to a lowered (opened port) position.

Awareness exercise 2: MOVING THE SOFT PALATE

1. Breathe in and out through your nose. Your mouth can be open or closed so long as you are still breathing through your nose.
2. Now hum on 'ng' /ŋ/ as you breathe out. Make the 'ng' more forceful than the siren in Chapter 5.

3. Continuing to sing on 'ng', pinch your nostrils. Notice what happens to the sound; notice what happens to the breath. When you pinch your nose, the breath and sound will stop. This is a sign that you have opened the nasal port. The sound has stopped because your fingers are preventing it from coming out of the nose.
4. Repeat stages 1–3 and, immediately after pinching your nostrils, sing 'gEE' /giː/. Notice what happens this time: the pressure inside your nose releases, and the sound is able to come out of your mouth. This is a sign that you have closed your nasal port.

How does this happen? When you make the 'ng' your palate and tongue are in contact as shown in Diagram 2 on page 58. When you prepare for the 'g', both the tongue and palate move up and back until they are touching the back wall of the pharynx. This enables you to make the breath stop for this consonant. When you make the vowel, the tongue drops away from the soft palate as shown in Diagram 5, but the palate stays up against the back wall, closing off the nasal cavity.

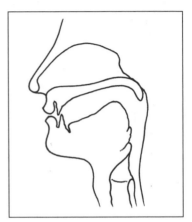

Diagram 5: Final stage of 'gEE'

Awareness exercise 3: WHAT MOVES WHERE?

You are using the same sounds and techniques as before but working more slowly.

1. Hum on 'ng' /ŋ/.
2. Gently pinch your nose as you continue to hum (the sound will stop).
3. Change the 'ng' to a 'g' and then sing on 'EE' /iː/ (so the whole sequence is 'ng'-'g'-'EE' /ŋgiː/). Notice what happens at each stage:
i.   as you begin with the 'ng' *your soft palate is down against your tongue*;
ii. as you prepare for the 'g' *your tongue and soft palate will move up together to touch the back wall of the pharynx* and the breath will stop;
iii. as you move from the 'g' to 'EE' *your tongue will drop away from the soft palate* and the breath will be released;
iv. as the make the vowel *your soft palate will stay up against the back wall.*

Sometimes the soft palate does not stay up and back when we move into the vowel. This means that the 'door' of the nasal port has been left partly open. To find out if you are doing this, use the nose pinch when singing the vowel 'EE'. If the sound changes and seems to switch partially on and off, you have left your nasal port partly open. See Exercise 3 on gaining control of the soft palate for work on the half-open nasal port.

Gaining control of the soft palate

Exercise 1: OPENING AND CLOSING

1. Say the sounds 'ng-gEE' /ŋgiː/. Make the 'g' moderately hard.
2. Repeat with sung notes, making a string of them 'ng-gEE - ng-gEE - ng-gEE - ng-gEE'.
   Notice that, as in the awareness exercises, there are changes in the airflow. Use the nose pinch to test when the nasal port is open and closed. Be aware of the total breath stop when you are preparing the 'g' and the sense of release when you move into the vowel.

Monitoring:
i. The jaw does not need to be moving up and down during this exercise. Either look in a mirror or monitor your jaw movement by putting a finger lightly on your chin. Keep the jaw still, and let the soft palate do the work.
ii. The muscles that make up the floor of the mouth, underneath your chin, need to be as soft as you can manage during this exercise. Avoid unnecessary muscle tension in this area. Monitor the soft part underneath your chin with your thumb as you go. Notice if you make a downward 'push' when you make the 'g', and try to soften this movement. This will help you to isolate the movement of the soft palate from the tongue.

Exercise 2: OPENING AND CLOSING WITH ALL VOWELS

Repeat Exercise 1 with other vowels from the vowel key on pages 42–3. Take your time, and make sure that you can close your port equally well on all the vowels. Use the monitoring devices as before.

Exercise 3: HALF-OPEN NASAL PORT

The aim of this exercise is to control the soft palate to the point where you can create nasal vowel sounds. This requires a balanced muscle use between the muscles that raise the soft palate and the muscles that depress it. You will be able to monitor by sound and feel when doing this exercise.

1. Make a conscious effort to sing down your nose as you say 'hEE'–'hEH'–'hAH'–'hAW'–'hOO' /hiː/ – /he/ – /hɑː/ – /hɔː/ – /huː/. You don't have to do the 'h', but it helps to direct first the breath and then the sound into the nose. The jaw position needs to be as before when you were monitoring. Notice the change in vowel quality and in resonance: the vowels will sound (and may feel) different and the resonance will be less 'bright'. Using your fingers, pinch and release the end of your nose as you hold the vowels. Notice that the sound now seems to partially switch on and off: partially 'off' when you pinch, more 'on' when you release. This effect is only possible if your nasal port is half-open. Look at Diagrams 2–4 again. Notice that it is possible for the sound to travel out of both the nose and the mouth. Remember the sound and feel of the half-open port as you continue with the next stage:

2. Begin with an open port singing 'ng'. You are aiming to move your soft palate just a little way from your tongue. The movement is in a very specific place. You will feel it at the back of your nose, where we were working in Awareness exercise 2.

3. This time do not make the transition from 'ng' to 'ng-g', but just glide into a vowel. It doesn't matter too much at this stage what the vowel is, though 'EE' is what we are aiming for eventually. Avoid going all the way up into the closed port position. Think of doing your previous closed port exercise rather lazily. Aim to match the sound quality with your half-open port sounds from stage 1 above. Use the nose-pinch to see if your port is half-open, repeating this manoeuvre several times.

Exercise 4: HALF-OPEN TO CLOSED NASAL PORT

The aim of this exercise is to find what changes when moving from a nasal to an oral vowel.

1. Sing on a nasalised 'EE' /ĩː/, using the techniques from Exercise 3. Once again, use the nose-pinch and feel the sensation of air coming into the nose.

2. Continue singing on 'EE', and aim to 'take the air out of the nose'. It doesn't matter if you don't know how this happens; simply follow the instruction.

3. Something has changed: the sound is usually louder on the 'EE', and the resonance is also different. The air can no longer be felt by your fingers at the end of the nose, which means you have closed the nasal port. You have now made the shift from half-open to closed port.

If you cannot close your nasal port efficiently when you are singing, you may lose a considerable amount of resonance. The oral cavity is a more efficient resonator than the nasal cavity as it is bigger, and it has less soft tissue and other substances that will dampen the sound. With oral resonance the sound will be brighter and often louder. So, acoustically, it makes sense to sing with the nasal port closed. There are other specific benefits to gaining control of the nasal port:

1. You cannot form the vowels properly if the port is open. There are only three sounds in Standard English that are made with the nasal port open: 'n' /n/, 'm' /m/ and 'ng' /ŋ/. Everything else needs to be done with the nasal port closed.

2. In Standard American speech there is a higher degree of nasality than in Standard British, particularly on the vowels 'AH' /ɑː/ and 'AW' /ɔː/. In singing American, you may choose to form the vowels with the nasal port closed to produce a more vibrant tone.

3. Some performers have difficulty with breath control if they habitually sing with the nasal port open. This is because they get used to the sensation of vibration in the nasal cavity during singing. With the breath being diverted into two places while singing vowels, breath use is more likely to be inefficient.

4. Some regional accents feature a half-open port on consonants other than the usual nasal ones. Singers with these speech patterns should pay particular attention to the nasal port exercises.

5. Being aware of the effort involved in raising the soft palate can be helpful in easy access to top notes. See Exercise 5, stage 1:vi.

These are the circumstances under which the nasal port will be open in singing:

1. It needs to be totally open for 'n', 'm' and 'ng'. Every time you sing a word containing one of these consonants (for example 'and'), your nasal port will be closed then opening as you sing it. (See Song Assignment 4 at the end of this chapter for practice in singing syllables with nasal consonants.)

2. Humming exercises on 'm'.

3. In some circumstances you can use nasal port opening to make a decrescendo in singing. See Exercise 7 on page 67.

4. Nasality can be used as a conscious choice in vocal quality. The reasons might be stylistic or interpretive.

Before moving on to work on application of the techniques, here is a summary of the cues we have been using for monitoring control of the soft palate:

Monitoring control of the soft palate

Port Open: the nasal consonants 'ng', 'm' and 'n'. You will feel the sound and breath coming down your nose when you make them. The sound and breath will stop when you pinch your nostrils. The sound quality is, by definition, nasal.

Port Closed: the vowels of Standard British and American. There is no change when you do the nostril pinch. The sound quality is by definition oral, and it is heard as more 'open'.

Port half-open: nasalized vowels. The sound is resonating in both the nose and the mouth cavities. When you do the nostril pinch, the sound changes. The vowel quality is corrupted, and the sound may be heard as 'dull' or 'flat' compared with the closed port position.

Exercises in Application

For the next two exercises find a start note from a keyboard or other instrument, or work with an accompaniment.

Exercise 5: OPENING AND CLOSING THE NASAL PORT WHILE SINGING SCALES

1. On a descending scale sing 'ng-gEE' /ŋgiː/ thus:

ng-gEE ng-gEE ng-gEE ng-gEE   ng-gEE ng-gEE ng-gEE ng-gEE

You will be opening and closing the nasal port on each note.
Be aware of the following:

i.   The work is done at the back of the mouth, so keep your jaw relaxed. Use the jaw monitoring device as before: either look into a mirror or place your finger on your chin.

ii. The tongue and soft palate need to be together to make the 'ng' /ŋ/.

iii. If you are able to raise the back of the tongue towards the soft palate (rather than lowering the palate towards the tongue), it will help you in preparing for the 'g'. The tip of the tongue needs to be out of the way and positioned behind the bottom front teeth. If your tongue is short or has a short tie, you may not be able to do this. In this case, allow the tip of the tongue to relax and drop when you prepare to make the 'g'.

iv. In moving from the 'g' to 'EE' /giː/ make the action energetic.

v. Watch out for constriction. Nasal port closure is a preparation for swallowing, so remember to retract the false vocal folds.

vi. If you are used to 'making space' for high notes, you will want to stop doing the 'ng' as you ascend in pitch. Avoid separating the palate and tongue as you go higher; keep raising the back of the tongue towards the soft palate as you go up in pitch, even if it feels 'tight'.

vii. Notice if you are lazy with your soft palate as you go to the bottom of your range. Some singers will lower the palate if they are thinking 'down'; keep the work in the 'g' moderately hard as before.

Do this sequence as slowly as you need to to begin with, taking small top-up breaths at any point. Most people need a lot of thinking time for this exercise; you can increase the speed later.

Over and again, I have found that teaching this exercise, in addition to controlling the nasal port, enables easy access to the top of the range.

2. Now repeat the sequence on any combination of vowels in turn ('ng-gAH' 'ng-gAW' 'ng-gOO', /ŋgɑː/ /ŋgɔː/ /ŋguː/, or on all the vowels.

Watch out for the following:

i. Make sure you can close your port equally well on all the vowels. Even with the back vowels where the back of the tongue is high – for example, 'OO' /uː/ – you can still get a closed port.

ii. Remember to round the lips on 'AW' /ɔː/, 'aw' /ɒ/, and 'OO' /uː/.

Once you have mastered these stages and can increase your speed, move onto the next stage, which should be done at speed.

3. Ascend the scale, going through a full octave singing through five vowels at a time and taking a breath whenever you need it.

ng-gEE ng-gEH ng-gAH ng-gAW ng-gOO   ng-gEE ng-gEH ng-gAH etc

This is a wonderful exercise for coordinating the action of the muscles in the oral cavity: muscles of the palate, lips and tongue. Remember to monitor your jaw by looking in a mirror or by placing a finger on your chin. The jaw needs to be passive in this exercise.

Many singers experience a sensation of lifting when they want to access higher pitches and increase resonance. In the exercise that follows, you might well get a sense of extra uplift around the area of your soft palate. In addition to helping you access a more vibrant tone, you will find it helpful in accessing top notes.

Diagram 6 on page 66 shows a view of the mouth and palate from the front. You can see that there are two arches at the back of the mouth; the one deepest inside is the palato pharyngeus. If the soft palate is stabilised, the palato pharyngeus can shorten the pharynx (back wall of the vocal tract) and so assist us in finding top notes.

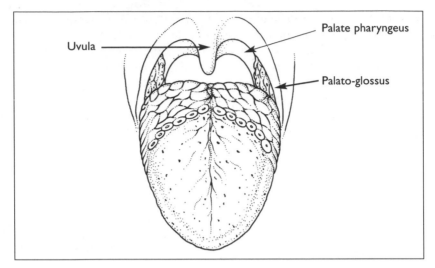

Diagram 6: Front view of the oral cavity

Exercise 6: PALATO PHARYNGEUS AND THE 'LIFT'

In this exercise, you are looking for a sensation of effort deep to the soft palate. It will feel like something happening behind the nose and above the roof of the mouth.

1. At a slow speed, open and close the nasal port by singing: 'ng-gEE' /ŋgiː/. Pinch your nostrils when you reach the vowel.
2. Still singing 'EE' /iː/, keep hold of the nose and try to 'pull' harder where you felt the port close; notice that the sound becomes fuller and more resonant. Make a note of where you feel the effort and how hard you are working.
3. Now take your fingers away from the nose.
4. Repeat the sequence, gliding into other vowels from the 'EE': 'ng-gEE-eh-AH-AW-OO' /ŋgiːeɑːɔːuː/.
   Watchpoints:
   i. Monitor constriction; silently laugh at the larynx.
   ii. Keep the jaw out of the act; if it is tense, do a little chewing while you are singing.
   iii. Do not tense your tongue; roll it around inside the mouth if it is tensing unnecessarily.
   iv. Do not try to sing louder; this increase in sound does not happen in the vocal folds. It is probably a result of improving your vocal tract resonance.
5. Practise the sequence again without the nostril pinching.

You could use this muscular sensation of 'lift' in Exercise 5 when approaching your top notes.

Exercise 7: MAKING A DECRESCENDO WITH THE SOFT PALATE

Closing the port can give you increased volume by changing the resonance, and conversely you can decrease volume by opening the port. This change in volume is due to the nasal cavity damping down some of the harmonics.

1. Sing the vowel 'EE' /iː/, checking that the nasal port is closed by pinching the nostrils as you sing.
2. Keeping everything else exactly the same, gradually lower your soft palate towards the tongue as if going to make an 'ng' /ŋ/.
3. Stop before you get to the 'ng' and hold this position. You may find it difficult at first to coordinate stopping halfway. Practise a few times. When you are successful, you will be producing a nasalised 'EE' /ĩː/.
4. Now do the same manoeuvre slowly singing the word 'end'. Sing the vowel for as long as you can, making a gradual transition to the nasal 'n' before the final 'd'.

/e/ – /ẽ/ – /n/ – /n/ – /d/

If you are doing ensemble work and cannot sing softly enough for the musical director, you may find this helpful in making a decrescendo. This works well for words ending in nasal consonants. Be aware that the sound quality as well as the volume will change, make sure that you are able to hold your pitch. In Chapter 7 we shall be looking at other ways to change volume.

Mirening

'Mirening' is a made-up word meaning to mouth at the front and siren on 'ng' /ŋ/ at the back. Actors often rehearse forming the vowels and consonants silently to practise articulation skills and to embed muscular memory of text. Mirening forms the link between shaping the vowels and consonants and pitching the notes in sung text. When you add the sirening dimension to silent text work, you'll find that you can still shape all of the consonants except for those that are made with the palate, such as 'k' /k/ and 'g' /g/. If you 'think' the vowel shape even while making the 'ng' /ŋ/ your tongue will make minor adjustments in preparation for each vowel. You can use your lips for the round vowels in the normal way.

Song assignments

Song assignment 1: MIRENING

1. Look at the words and melody from the beginning of '*The way you look tonight*' by Jerome Kern. Rehearse them silently, taking care to form the vowels and consonants accurately.

2. Next sing the whole melody to 'ng' /ŋ/as in sirening.
3. Put stages 1 and 2 together, singing the melody on 'ng' and mouthing the words with the tongue and lips. All that will be heard is the 'ng', but you will be moving the muscles of articulation; you will feel the changes for different vowel shapes and for the consonants bar the velar consonants 'g' /g/ and 'k' /k/.

Mirening requires considerable coordination. It will help you to coordinate the muscles that control articulation with the muscles that make the pitch. It is extremely useful in song-learning.

Song assignment 2: YOUR SONG

1. Work with the song that you chose for the Song Assignment at the end of Chapter 5. Record yourself doing the following routines:
i.   singing the song once through;
ii. mirening the song; remember to keep the 'ng' /ŋ/ at the back of the mouth all the way through this part of the exercise;
iii. singing the song with a half-open nasal port.
     You will probably find that the half-open port singing takes a lot of breath. This doesn't matter. Just do the exercise and notice what you feel.
2. Listen back to the recording. You will probably notice that the half-open port affected your tuning as well as your breath use. There is less resonance when the port is open, and it can make your tuning flat. You'll also notice that the vowels have less 'presence'.

Song assignment 3: HAPPY BIRTHDAY

'*Happy Birthday*' has no nasal consonants in it provided you sing the third line as 'happy birthday, happy birthday'. It's also a song that covers a range of one octave and so can be used as an exercise, going up or down in key.
1. Test your ability to close the nasal port by singing the whole song with your fingers just touching underneath the nostrils. If the port is closed, you should feel no air coming down the nose.
2. Practise the song in different keys, i.e. from different starting notes in your range.

Song assignment 4: AMAZING GRACE

Most songs do have words with nasal consonants in them. The aim of this assignment is to identify what happens with the soft palate when we sing these words. Let's look at the first phrase of '*Amazing Grace*':

A - m - az - ing _____ Grace, how   sweet   the   sound

The nasal consonants are underlined. Each time you sing one of these, the nasal port needs to open; when you go into the vowel that follows, the port needs to close up again.
1. Sing this phrase slowly, making sure that the sound really is coming down the nose for the sounds 'm', 'n' and 'ng' /ŋ/. Pinch the nostrils to check.
2. As you approach each of these nasal consonants and as you come out of them, check that the nasal port is closed.
   It is not uncommon to start opening the port when a syllable ends with a nasal consonant. In speech this is called co-articulation, where the vowel takes on some of the quality of the following consonant. Because singing is sustained pitch, you need to be aware of grading this transition from the oral vowel to the nasal consonant. This is more advanced work, which we will examine in Chapter 11. When working on this song assignment, keep the nasal port closed until you are ready to make the consonant.
3. Each time you learn a new song, mark in the nasal consonants, either using the phonetic symbol ~ or a sign that you have invented for yourself.

I would like to end the chapter by revisiting those misconceptions from page 59.

1. *'The soft palate is always up when you are singing.'* It may feel like something is lifting, but it won't be the soft palate if you are singing on 'm', 'n' and 'ng' /ŋ/.

2. *'The soft palate lifts automatically when you breathe in.'* This is the case if you breathe in through your mouth only.

3. *'You have no independent control over the soft palate.'* This is not true; you can develop control over the soft palate.

4. *'You will get a brighter tone if you sing into your nose.'* This is the case, only if you are using nasal twang, otherwise the sound will be duller. The oral cavity is a more efficient resonator than the nasal cavity.

5. *'The contemporary musical theatre sound is nasal.'* Sometimes this is the case, but mostly what is heard in contemporary musical theatre is due to twang, not nasality. More of twang in Chapter 9.

The work in this chapter has been necessarily intricate, requiring you to really focus on specific muscle groups. The pay-off is that you will not only gain more control, but you will also find a greater freedom. Many singer and actors hunt for space and freedom in their vocal production. All kinds of imagery are used to help find these spaces. By focusing on the soft palate in the upper part of the vocal tract and the false vocal folds in the lower part you will go a long way towards opening up your voice.

Chapter 7

Dynamic control and projection

In this chapter we shall be looking at dynamic control – how to increase and decrease volume – and at the concept of muscular support or 'voice-body connection'. It is a favourite question of mine in workshops to ask 'how do we get louder?' The answers are sometimes interesting and usually include 'making more space', 'lowering my larynx', 'more blade' and (nearly always) 'more breath'. It is rare for anyone to mention increased work in the vocal folds.

Let's consider what constitutes effortless loud voice or projection.

HIGH INTENSITY VOCALISATION

In order to be loud and project well a voice needs to generate good vocal fold vibration (for the fundamental) and a good balance of harmonic energy, which is heard as voice quality. In addition to this, vocal and physical effort needs to be balanced so that the production is seemingly effortless. Three factors contribute to increased loudness:

1. The movement of the vocal folds will be wide and free. The vocal folds need to come together quickly when closing, and move further apart when opening. This more energetic movement of the vocal folds will give both the strong fundamental and the harmonic energy needed for effortless loud singing.

2. Sub-glottic pressure and airflow will increase because of the wider movement in the vocal folds.

3. Retraction assists the vocal folds in achieving the wide free movement required for loud singing.

In order to get louder (or softer) there has to be a change in the vocal folds as well as in the breath. In Chapter 4, you worked a number of exercises that enabled you to create and maintain the sub-glottic pressure needed for loud singing. What happens in the vocal folds to assist changes in volume?

Look at Diagrams 1–3 of your vocal folds in three different modes of vibration. The view is of your vocal folds from the front, as if a slice has been made through the top of your head face on.

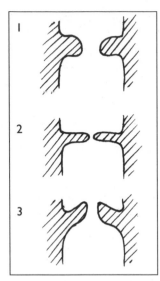

The vocal folds – 1 – thick;
2 – thin; 3 – raised plane

These diagrams will help you to visualise what is happening inside as you go through the exercises that follow. A complex inter-action between the muscles of the vocal folds (*vocalis*) and muscles of the larynx enable the vocal folds to vibrate differently. Thicker folds (Diagram 1) will tend to give us a louder sound; thinner folds (Diagrams 2 and 3) will tend to give us a softer sound; vocal folds in the raised plane position (Diagram 3) do not meet and therefore have no 'closed phase'. This mode is not suitable for loud sounds.

It is challenging sometimes to decon-struct sound production. It is natural that both the vocalist and the listener will experience everything happening as one. Deconstruction has been a feature of work in this book so far. As we progress to more advanced work, it will be necessary to revisit some topics, layering them to make a whole. Here is a more advanced version of the onset and breath work that we did in Chapters 2 and 4; it will enable you to clarify the relationship between effort levels in the vocal folds and effort levels in the breath during loud and soft singing.

Effort levels in the breath and vocal folds

Awareness exercise 1: THICK FOLDS

1. Work some voiced fricatives in spoken voice from the exercises in Chapter 4 pages 30–1. This will help you to build up sub-glottic pressure and to close the vocal folds for loud voicing.
2. Work several fricatives in one breath, using the diamond of support (see pages 31–2).
3. Using 'heys' and 'yeahs', call out in spoken voice on different pitches, keeping your sense of work in the abdominal muscles.
4. Now move on to sung pitches, this time using the 'uh-oh' from Chapter 2 page 15 and Chapter 4 page 37. Use the muscle memory of the voiced fricatives to allow you to build up breath before the glottal closure.
5. Repeat stage 4; this time hold the final 'oh' as a sung pitch.
6. Repeat the sequence, experimenting with different vowels and pitches,

('EE-EE' /iː/, 'ae-ae' /æ/ and so on), then singing the words of a song on one note.

You have now found an increased work level identified as 'thick folds'. You will probably feel a greater sense of connection between your voice and breath, and the sound will be relatively loud.

Monitoring effort levels:
i. Monitor your breath pressure; it needs to balance with the task. Avoid giving your vocal folds too much breath to resist or you may push your voice.
ii. Monitor constriction in the larynx by using the silent laugh.
iii.Do the exercise on comfortable pitches to begin with. We will address range later.

Awareness exercise 2: THIN FOLDS

This explores the opposite extreme from Awareness exercise 1.
1. Get ready to do a siren by whining, whimpering or moaning softly. A further auditory cue is a thoughtful 'mm' that you might make while listening to someone talk on the phone (the motivation is 'I'll need to think about that...'). Make the same quality of sound on an 'ng'.
2. Using the same low effort levels in volume and breath, move from making an 'ng' into vowel sounds. Do this in spoken voice first.
3. Now sing a pitch, starting with the 'ng' and moving into vowels: 'ng–EE–eh–AH–AW–OO' /ŋiːeɑːɔːuː/, aiming to keep the sound as soft as you can.
4. Monitor what is happening with your breathing. How much breath is needed to make the sound? How long are you able to hold the notes?
5. Repeat the sequence, experimenting with different vowels and pitches, then singing the words of a song as one note.

You have now found an alternative setting in the larynx for thinner vocal folds. The sound will be softer but will still carry well, because the vocal folds are meeting on thinned edges.

Monitoring effort levels:
i. Surprisingly, soft singing is energetic. Monitor constriction by using the silent laugh.
ii. Aim to do a controlled release of your breath by working slowly and gently with your abdominal wall.
iii.Remember to recoil at the ends of notes.

Auditory and visual monitoring

This is a good point to stop to do some comparative work, exploring what it is like to move from thick folds to thin folds. With a partner you could do some listening exercises. Alternatively, physicalising your sound, using hand or whole body movements, could help you to develop muscle memory for thin and thick vocal folds. Notice the change in dynamic: thicker folds give a louder sound, and thinner folds give a softer sound. Comparative work will help you to realise that there are effort levels between thin and thick that can be found via more subtle changes. The dynamic from softer to louder will alter accordingly.

Awareness exercise 3: RAISED VOCAL FOLD PLANE

We are now revisiting work from Chapter 3, pages 25–6. The muscles that enable us to raise the vocal fold plane are the same ones that open the vocal folds for breathing.

1. Vocalise a sigh or yawn, starting on a medium to high pitch in your range. Make sure you start the sound with an 'h'. (Another useful auditory cue for this posture is a very English 'yoo-hoo'.)
2. Do this several times until you are sure that you have found the 'raised plane' position from Chapter 3, page 25.
3. Speak in this mode, using words or vowel sounds.
4. Sing the line of a song, without changing either the sound quality or the 'feel'.
5. Explore getting louder and softer in raised plane mode. Notice changes in your breath use and in the sound quality, often described as 'hooty' or hollow.

   In the raised plane position the vocal folds generally do not meet, so there is very little resistance to the breath. There is nothing wrong with this sound quality, but it does not project well and is low in harmonic energy.

Monitoring effort levels:

i. How easy or hard does it feel to make this sound?
ii. How would you describe the sense of connection between the breath and the voice?

Auditory and visual monitoring can be used here as before, this time for comparing all three modes.

The chart opposite gives a useful summary of the work you have been doing on effort levels in the breath and vocal folds.

Changes in the vocal folds

- *Thicker vocal folds:* louder sounds. There is increased work in the vocal folds and muscles of active expiration.
- *Thinner vocal folds:* softer sounds. The vocal folds are elongated and tensed; the breath is more 'controlled'.
- *Raised vocal fold plane:* softer sounds. The vocal folds are open though vibrating, and breath use is inefficient. This is unsuitable for loud sounds.
- Thin to thick folds will give a gradual dynamic change.

ANCHORING, THE VOICE-BODY CONNECTION

The vocal folds on their own are not enough to enable seemingly effortless projection in large spaces or over long-term use. Even with the aid of sufficient sub-glottic pressure, the workload may be too great for these tiny and delicate muscles. Anchoring[1] provides support via a muscular voice-body connection. It is not the same as breath support. For centuries voice trainers from both singing and speaking traditions have employed other strategies that enabled them to access louder sounds to 'fill' spaces safely. We are going to look at some of these strategies now. Later, in Chapter 9, we will look at the other essential element for projection: 'the singer's formant' or 'twang'.

Vocal tract anchoring

The larynx is a suspensory mechanism; it needs to be highly mobile so that we can swallow food. Since it is not attached directly or indirectly to the spinal column we need to stabilise it via other muscles. By working muscles in the vocal tract around the larynx we can lend support to its work against the oncoming breath. Anchoring the vocal tract also has the effect of increasing resonance. Changes in head and neck posture give a sensation of 'more room'; also muscle and soft tissue that make up the oral cavity are firmed up giving a more resonant surface.

There are two key points about anchoring:

1. The greater the vocal task, the harder you may need to work to support the vibrating mechanism.

2. Isolation is essential to anchoring.

---

[1] Anchoring is a term used by Estill in her *Compulsory Figures for Voice.*

Isolation checklist

1. Laugh silently to retract the false vocal folds.
2. Release the abdominal wall so that you can breath in and out easily – check this by saying the voiced fricatives 'v' and 'z' while you are anchored and recoil with the breath between each sound. You can then breathe normally.
3. Relax the mouth, jaw and the tongue by chewing and rolling the tongue around inside the mouth.
4. Adjust your posture and move around freely.
5. Siren quietly or make small sounds on vowels to check you are not transferring too much work onto the vocal folds.

The following exercises can be done without sound to begin with. This will enable you to locate and work the muscle groups that support your voice. Remember to use the *Isolation Checklist* when you work the muscles. Each exercise can then be repeated adding sounds, using the siren, vowels and lines of songs. The vocal tract can be stabilised from behind, from the sides and front, and from inside.

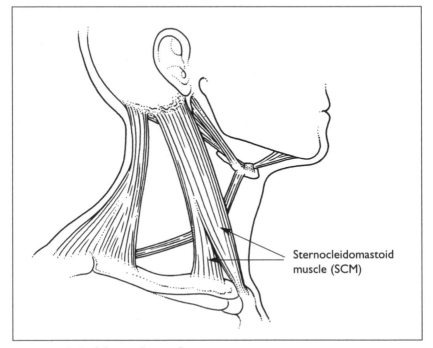

Sternocleidomastoid muscle (SCM)

Diagram 4: Stabilising the vocal tract

Diagrams 4 and 5 indicate the muscle groups that are likely to be working to stabilise the vocal tract from outside. Muscles tend to work together, so do not expect to be able to isolate individual muscles. Aim for a sensation of balanced effort.

Exercise I: EXTERNAL ANCHORING

Here are four devices for exploring external anchoring.

1. Work to straighten the cervical spine by lengthening and pulling slightly back. Feel for the larger bump of the atlas joint with one hand and the axis joint with the other. Aim to bring these joints into line. Take your hands away, and keep the anchored position for the neck.

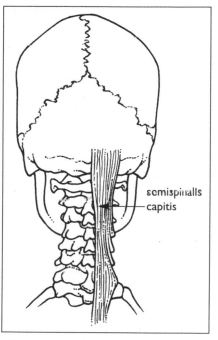

semispinalls
capitis

Diagram 5: Stabilising the vocal tract

2. The head pat. Put the palm of your hand flat on the crown of your head. Push down a little with your hand and push up a little with your head, keeping the neck in line with your spine. Again, remove the hand and maintain the muscle engagement.
3. Imagine putting on a tight olympic swimmer's cap. As you pull it onto your head, push your head up into the cap. Keep the sense of the lengthened neck once the cap is 'on'.
4. Feel for the big muscles around the side of your neck shown in Diagram 4 (the 'SCMs'). Put one hand around the sides of the neck near the front; make the other hand into a fist, which you put against the forehead. Keeping the back of the neck lengthened, press the fist against the forehead and push back against the fist with the forehead until you can feel the SCMs beginning to work.

Monitoring

i. Aim to keep the work isolated in the head and neck area only; you do not need to involve the shoulders, and you do not need to clamp the jaw.

ii. When you lengthen one part of your spine, something must happen in the rest of it. Do the exercise seated to begin with, making sure that your back is in alignment.

iii. When you come to practise this exercise standing up, avoid locking the knees and notice what is happening with your lumbar spine. Are you over-arching your back (sticking your behind out)? Or are you letting your pelvis slump forward, collapsing the lower back? Imagine a plumb line running down through the centre of your body, from the top of the skull down through the balls of the feet.

iv. Use a mirror, face and sideways on for visual feedback, or with a partner to get kinaesthetic feedback. Devices 1 and 2 can be done with a partner.

Make sure that you listen to your body when you do these exercises. They are about using resistance to get muscles working. Using the *Isolation Checklist*, make sure that you can now release inappropriate tensions and keep specific muscle groups working.

Auditory monitoring:
Use your singing and speaking voices for auditory monitoring.
i.   Speak or sing 'EE' /iː/ on a comfortable pitch and with a neutral stance, that is, not anchored.
ii. Stabilise your voice by using any of the anchoring devices described in Exercise 1. Aim to work the back and sides of the vocal tract, assigning an effort level to the muscular effort on a scale of 1–10.
iii. Repeat stage ii using the siren, other vowels, and lines of spoken and sung text.

Make a note of changes in volume and tonal quality. Your tone may well have got louder, apparently on its own. It will also have altered in another way, perhaps sounding 'wider' or 'fuller'. This will be due to increased resonance.

Kinaesthetic monitoring:
Describe the new sensation that you associate with the anchored tone. Examples might be 'stable', 'solid', 'dense', 'buzzy', 'full', 'free', 'flowing' and so on. It is common to feel that your voice comes out effortlessly when you use the anchoring devices.

Exercise 2: INTERNAL ANCHORING

Look at Diagram 6 to help you visualise where you will feel the muscles working in this exercise. Once again, there will be a series of cues to help you locate the muscles and get them working. As before, use the *Isolation Checklist* after engaging effort each time.

1. Imagine the smell of something you really want to eat or drink, or of a favourite place such as a pine forest or the ozone-filled atmosphere at the seashore. Activate your sense of smell and widen the nostrils. Hold the muscular effort, release the jaw, and breathe out silently through the mouth.

2. Imagine biting into a small, crisp apple or other favourite fruit that is firm. Hold the feeling of the bite in your upper jaw and release it from the lower jaw.

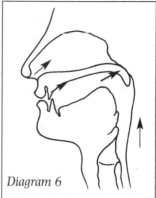

Diagram 6

3. Sucking either a real or imaginary straw, pretend that the straw is blocked at the bottom end so that nothing is coming up. Hold the muscular effort, release the jaw, and breathe out silently through the mouth.

All of the devices above work muscles inside the vocal tract. The muscles of the soft palate will be activated, as well as the back wall of the vocal tract.

As with the external anchoring devices, use devices 1–3 with spoken and sung voice and listen out for changes in volume and tonal quality. It is really helpful to do this with someone else listening. There is a marked difference in resonance, probably due to an increase in harmonic energy. These exercises have been called variously 'bringing the voice forward', 'placing the voice', '*inhalare la voce*' (inhaling the tone), and 'using the mask of the voice'. None of them is about 'placing' your voice anywhere; they are simply about working the muscles of the vocal tract.

Monitoring:
i. These exercises can lead to you pulling strange faces if you do not isolate! Using a mirror, monitor your effort levels until you can still feel something working inside, but it is not obvious from outside.
ii. Check especially for jaw tension, bulging eyes and raised eyebrows.
iii.Remember to retract the false vocal folds: use an elastic band across your thumbs as a reminder, or spread your thumbs as described on page 46.

The exercises that follow target larger muscle groups in the body. Some of these muscles used to be called muscles of 'forced expiration', which means that they are useful in more forceful vocal tasks. You will find that they have an effect on your breath use generally, and they will enable you to make loud energetic sounds safely.

Torso Anchoring

Look at Diagrams 7 and 8 to help you locate the muscles we shall be using in torso anchoring.

Because of their attachments to the ribs, the spine, the diaphragm and the pelvis, these muscles will have the effect of stabilising the body – and hence the breath – during active voice work. Alexander work acknowledges the importance of stabilising the back of the torso so that the front can 'pull up' and the abdominal contents are moved back. These muscles are sometimes called muscles of forced expiration, implying an energetic expiration.

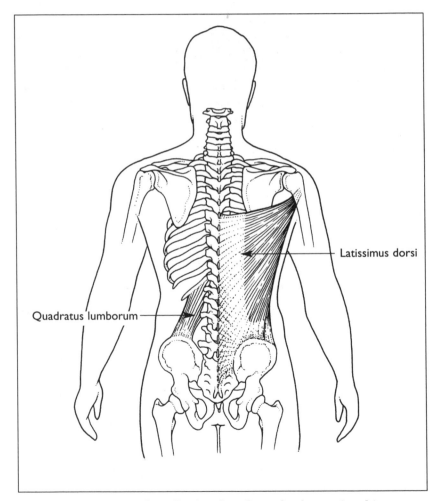

Diagram 7: Latissimus dorsi (lats) and quadratus lumborum (quads)

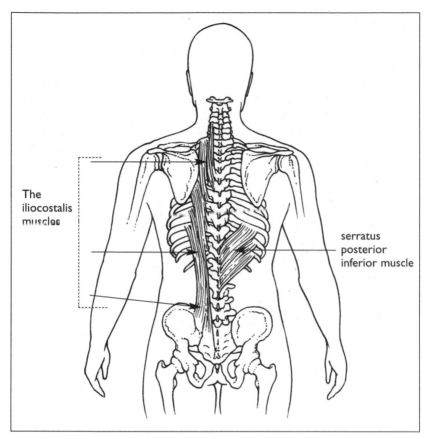

Diagram 8: Iliocostalis muscles and the serratus posterior

Exercise 3: ANCHORING THE TORSO

1. Stand easily with the feet comfortably apart and with the knees not locked.
i. Turn your arms in their sockets away from the body, keeping them close to you. This will fix the top of your lats.
ii. Keeping the lats fixed, engage the muscles to pull down and out, working from the armpits into the upper back.
2. Work with a partner. Your partner can put a hand each side into your armpits. You need to crook your elbows slightly so that you do not lock the arms.
i. Squeeze your partner's hands under your armpits, pulling down and out from the armpits as before.
ii. If you are ticklish, you can do this exercise against a semi-soft ball tucked under your armpit.

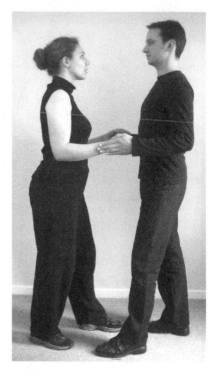

Photograph 1: Body balancer   *Photograph 2: Pushing hands*

3. This is 'the body balancer'. Look at Photograph 1, which shows two people working to find the anchoring muscles together. You should be a comfortable distance apart with a good neutral stance. Each person needs to make sure that their spine is in a line with their neck and pelvis, and that the shoulders are dropped and the knees not locked.

i. Take it in turns to pull, one against the other. Keep your elbows close to your body with the arms not locked.

ii. Whoever is anchoring needs to avoid pulling with the arms. The work is in the back of the body. Tell yourself to simply 'take the elbows backwards'.

iii. Your partner needs to be sensitive and create just enough resistance to activate the muscles. If there is too much, you will both lock.

4. Look at Photograph 2. Note that person A is pushing outwards and person B is pushing inwards. Keep the elbows in line with the body and at roughly shoulder width. Avoid locking the arms. Again, be sensitive to each other when engaging effort.

Monitoring effort:
Always use the *Isolation Checklist* with the torso anchoring devices. It is essential that you are able to retract the false vocal folds and free up the abdominal wall at the front so that you can do the recoil breath. Explore different levels of effort using the number system. It is good to feel work, but there should be no pain or discomfort. If you do the exercises and you experience either of these, check your general posture.

Auditory monitoring:
As with the vocal tract anchoring (Exercise 2), you can now add sound. Use small sounds to begin with, then increase the breath pressure and the work in the vocal folds so that you can build volume. Use spoken and sung voice. Explore the difference with the same notes, and sung or spoken lines of text, with and without the anchoring. If you are working with a partner, find the anchored position, maintain your effort levels, and move away from your partner, still anchoring as you sing notes or lines of sung text.

You will also find the torso anchoring exercises useful when you produce high-energy voice qualities, such as belting, and when you are singing something very sustained. Anchoring in the torso enables you to put heavy demands on your voice safely. I have consistently found that people with big voices need to use a degree of torso anchoring all the time. There is something about the sheer physicality of big voices that demands this amount of input to make a decent sound. Big voices can be difficult to control. As a consequence the singer tends to hold back, sometimes constricting and de-voicing. If you suspect you are one of these people, you need to use torso anchoring as a matter of course.

EFFORTLESS PROJECTION

So-called effortless projection is actually a result of several factors:
1. Work in the vocal folds;
2. Work in the breath;
3. Work to open the false vocal folds;
4. Work to stabilise the larynx;
5. Work to maximise resonance.

These are what we hear when someone has a 'good' voice. Now *you* have the knowledge to put these components together.

Application

There are many situations in which you would apply work in the vocal folds described at the beginning of this chapter (pages 71–5), and work in the anchoring muscles (pages 75–83). Probably the most obvious of these is to increase tone. 'Tone' can mean both volume and quality, the latter being necessarily somewhat subjective. However, as a rule of thumb, these are the options for increasing tone:

1. Change to a thicker fold 'mass';
2. Increase work in the anchoring muscles;
3. Use strategies 1 and 2 together;
4. Use the 'singer's formant' or twang.

In addition to this, you will find the anchoring strategies useful when negotiating gear changes in your range. The anchoring helps to stabilise your larynx during these awkward change points. Anchoring will also have an effect on your breath use, enabling you to sustain for longer. Anchoring can also be used for quiet singing; it is not just about volume. Many singers speak about the work involved in quiet singing. This is because a very fine balance is needed between thinned vocal folds and a controlled release of air. You can use the vocal tract anchoring separately from the torso anchoring, but I never teach the torso anchoring without first straightening the cervical spine (see stages 1 and 2 of Exercise 1) as this would unbalance the body. Anchoring is also great for stage fright. It is not uncommon to feel breathless and as if you are losing your voice when you have stage fright. Use the vocal tract anchoring exercises when this happens to you, silently anchoring and breathing out slowly at the same time. Then add the siren, so that voicing is reintroduced. I have used this successfully with students in drama colleges waiting to go on for their final showcase, and I have used it with actors who were losing their voice mid-run.

Further exercises applying work from this chapter follow. These are the '*messa di voce*' (for dynamic control), working the range (for negotiating the gear changes), further work on gear changes, and one song assignment.

Exercise 4: MESSA DI VOCE OR DYNAMIC CONTROL

Essentially this is an exercise in getting louder and quieter, working both the vocal folds and the anchoring muscles. Musically, it's depicted by the hairpins:

1. Sing quietly on 'ng' /ŋ/ using 'thin' vocal folds.
2. Still singing quietly, peel your soft palate away from the tongue: 'ng-EE' /ŋiː/ until you have closed the nasal port.
3. Gradually increase your vocal fold mass while stabilising the vocal tract (from the back, sides and inside). You may need to increase your airflow as well, so monitor the abdominals.

4. Anchor the torso as you get louder still. Remember to use the silent laugh.
5. Stop when you have reached your maximum comfortable loudness level (effortless projection).
6. Now reverse the process. Still singing 'EE' /iː/, gradually reduce the effort level in the vocal folds until you have reached 'thin' folds.
7. Keep some effort in the anchoring muscles, and maintain your silent laugh. Notice that, as you get quieter, you are using less air and working with the anchoring muscles to control the breath.

With practice you can do this faster in one manoeuvre and in one breath.

Exercise 5: WORKING THE RANGE

1. Start on a low note, and siren up an octave on a quiet 'ng' /ŋ/.
2. Still holding the top note, peel your soft palate away from the back of the tongue to make an 'EE' /iː/.

3. Now add vocal tract anchoring. Use the devices that work for you. Work the diamond of support if you feel the need for more breath for your vocal folds to resist.
i. Make sure you have retracted the false vocal folds.
ii. Close your nasal port for the 'EE'.
iii. Pay attention to your posture; the spine should be in alignment and the shoulders relaxed. Your feet need to be comfortably apart at about hip width and the knees not locked.
    If you have done all this correctly, there will have been an increase in volume and tone (resonance) on the top note as you held it.
4. Repeat the sequence and come back down the octave on 'EE', keeping the new dynamic level.
5. Work through your entire range like this and on all the vowels.

Do not go faster than thinking speed to begin with. Once you are sure of what you are doing you can increase your working speed.

GEAR CHANGES, RANGE AND VOCAL REGISTERS

You will commonly hear singers and teachers of singing refer to different vocal 'registers'. Some singing teachers use the word 'register' as though it is interchangeable with 'range', for example 'upper and lower' register. As discussed in Chapter 1, the vocal registers often mentioned are 'chest', and 'head' or 'falsetto'. The fact that head and falsetto are used interchangeably by some and not by others is very confusing. Still, the terms are in use, and we need some way of understanding what they might mean.

Gear changes, sometimes referred to as *passaggi*, are a natural response of the vocal folds to the need for increased vibrations required for higher pitches. Here are some examples of the frequency measurements for four different pitches. In singing the A below middle C, the vocal folds of both men and women must close and open *220 times a second*. In order to

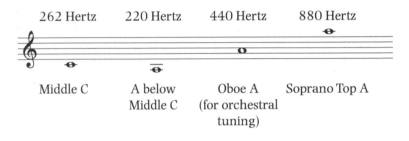

vibrate faster for higher pitches the vocal folds usually must change mass (thickness), either becoming more lax (relaxed) and slightly longer, or more tensioned and lengthened. This gear change is simply the transition point where changes of vocal fold mass occur. Speakers and singers of both sexes tend to change gear between the D and G above middle C. So this gear change happens roughly a third of the way up through the female voice range and two-thirds of the way up through the male voice range. There is a second gear change, which usually happens further up in the range. This change marks the need for the larynx to rise in order to stabilise for higher pitches. Muscles that assist in this gear change are the soft palate and the tongue, along with muscles that help to raise the larynx (laryngeal raisers). During sirening, this second gear change happens in the female voice between the upper D and F (a ninth and an eleventh above middle C). During sirening, it will happen in the male voice around the middle D and G as before. It is easy for one gear change to mask the other in the male voice. In my experience both changes need to happen, even if they are relatively close together in the range. Until you become used to managing these gear changes your voice may crack or break. Changes such as adjusting the tensioning of the vocal folds or raising the larynx itself can make the mechanism temporarily unstable. Vocal tract anchoring can help here.

Exercise 6: THINNING THE VOCAL FOLDS TO ASCEND THE SCALE

Work through stages 1–3 of Exercise 5. As you ascend the scale, you may feel that you are beginning to push your voice. If you are having difficulty at this point in your range:
1. Thin the vocal folds by tilting the thyroid, and reduce your airflow.
2. Stabilise the vocal tract by lengthening and working the back and sides of the neck.
3. Anchor from the inside if you require more volume.

Exercise 7: RAISING THE LARYNX TO ASCEND THE SCALE

Work through stages 1–3 of Exercise 5. As you approach the top third of your range, the larynx needs to rise. Muscles that pull the larynx up also have connections to the soft palate muscles. If the soft palate is not securely raised, these muscle groups will compete with each other, often causing the nasal port to open. It is not uncommon to feel that your voice is blocked because of the constriction that results from this difficulty.
1. Keep the nasal port closed. Review the work we did in Chapter 6, Exercise 1 (page 59), on the nasal port to make a strong seal between the nose and mouth.
2. Make sure that you are allowing the larynx to rise. Review Chapter 3, Awareness exercise 3, (page 21), on raising and lowering the larynx.
3. Sing 'ng-gEE' /ŋgiː/ on any notes you are having difficulty with to get the muscles into position for the high notes.

Exercise 8: THICKENING THE FOLDS TO DESCEND THE SCALE

Work through Exercise 5. When you are descending the scale, you may lose power if you do not increase your vocal fold mass.
1. Release the tilt in the thyroid as you approach the change point. Maintain anchoring in the back and sides of the neck. Aim to release the tilt gradually if you want to disguise the transition. You may need to increase your breath pressure for the thicker folds.
2. Alternatively, stop singing as you approach the change point and say 'EE' /iː/, using a glottal onset. Then sing the pitch you were aiming for on the 'EE', still using the glottal onset.

Exercise 9: LOWERING THE LARYNX TO DESCEND THE SCALE

Problems in the descent are less common in my experience. However, if you are having trouble finding your way down when you work through Exercise 5:
1. Monitor your larynx from outside as described in Chapter 3 (pages 18–20) or look in a mirror.

2. Release the upward pull on your larynx as you approach the change point.
3. Maintain stability in the back of the neck.
4. Allow your focus on the anchoring to move into the vocal tract to maximise resonance.
5. Avoid opening the nasal port to negotiate the gear change.

Exercises 6 to 9 give you the tools you need to deal with gear changes in your voice as you go through the range. Depending on your choice of voice quality, the changes may happen in different parts of your range. This will be discussed in more detail in Chapter 12.

Song assignment: THE BALCONY SCENE (TONIGHT) – TONY AND MARIA (WEST SIDE STORY)

Women can start at the beginning of the sequence 'Tonight, tonight' and finish on 'And what was just a world is a star, Tonight', on a high F marked fortissimo. Men can start at 'Always you, every thought I'll ever know', and end on 'You and me'. On the way there is a high G that starts *piano* (soft) and must end *forte* (loud).
1. Sing the passage. Remember that you are not belting; check that you are singing with a tilted thyroid. (See Chapter 3, and also Chapter 12 for Cry quality.)
2. Siren and miren the passage, paying attention to maintaining the tilted thyroid and retraction in the larynx.
3. Still mirening, engage the vocal tract anchoring, checking yourself at the sides, front and back.
4. Pull up inside the head and behind the nose as we did in Chapter 6 (page 66). Even though you are mirening on 'ng' /ŋ/ and your port is open, you will experience an extra 'lift' around the palate. An effort number will help you find the muscle memory.
5. Now sing the passage with the words, keeping the anchoring in place. There will be a change in tonal quality and possibly in volume as well.
6. If you are having difficulty sustaining the long phrases, use a degree of torso anchoring to hold the breath back. Make sure that you recoil properly in the centre of your abdominal wall when you do take a breath.

Projection is a word that is sometimes used somewhat loosely. In singing pedagogy it usually refers to the ability of a voice to be heard above a full orchestra. In acting it usually refers to the actors ability to fill the space vocally. This description is more relevant to singing actors today who, for the most part, will be working with amplified sound. I have found that clients respond well to knowing what happens in the vocal folds to change volume, as well as in the breath and body. And it goes without saying that volume control includes the ability to sing softly with presence as well as loudly. Loudness is only part of the equation. Resonance is also important, as is a sense of bodily connection. Perhaps it is the latter that contributes to vocal 'presence'. I often say to clients 'more muscle, less breath'. Muscles do not need breath to work. Separate breath support from postural and muscular support and you will find your voice use improves and that you are on the way to 'effortless' projection.

Chapter 8

Tuning the oral resonator

Clients frequently ask why it is that they have difficulty singing on 'AH' /ɑː/. This may be a general problem, or something that happens in a certain part of the range or in the production of a particular voice quality. From the front, 'AH' looks as though it should be a good vowel to sing: the jaw and lips are relaxed with the tongue low and 'out of the way'. Acoustically 'EE' /iː/ is a more favourable vowel for singing. 'EE' is made by bringing the tongue forward and away from the back wall of the vocal tract, resulting in more space. By manipulating the tongue, the lips and the jaw, you can tune the oral cavity to enhance specific resonances. This chapter explores these structures and the effect they can have on resonating quality.

THE JAW

'The jaw is a willing slave.' I cannot remember where I first heard this, but it is something I frequently quote in workshops and masterclasses. Many singers fix their jaw position in the mistaken belief that this will help sound production. One also sees singer furiously 'mouthing' to articulate. Not only is this visually distracting, it is inefficient. Consonants are made by obstructing the vocal tract; over-opening the jaw makes it harder for the muscles of articulation to do their work. We shall be considering consonants in Chapter 11.

Mostly when we talk about the jaw in singing, we mean specifically the lower jaw or mandible. The mandible provides the lower frame for the oral resonator. Muscles connect the jaw to the hyoid bone (at the base of the tongue) and to the tongue itself. It is easy to see movements of the jaw from outside, but not the effect of them. Any movements we make with the jaw will alter the position of the tongue and, to a lesser extent, its shape. Effectively the larynx is suspended from the tongue via the hyoid bone, so jaw movements may also have a knock-on effect on the larynx. My experience as a teacher has been that this important relationship between the jaw, tongue and larynx is not always understood. You may find it useful to refer back to the exercises for laryngeal orienteering and the diagram on pages 18–20 (Awareness exercise 2 Chapter 3) to see and feel the structures we are discussing. Let's begin by dealing with what can be seen from outside: jaw tension.

Dealing with jaw tension

A tense jaw may be clamped, out of alignment, or pushing downwards to open. The muscles that are in place to raise the jaw are some of the most powerful in the body. We use them for chewing food, and they are necessarily strong. Muscles that actively lower the jaw are few, so jaw 'release' is mainly about allowing the joint of the jaw to work efficiently by suspending the lower jaw from the upper. Our conditioning to hold the jaw closed is very strong. Even tiny babies, who have not yet learned how to resist gravity, know how to close the jaw.

The exercises that follow will help you to recognise and monitor jaw tension.

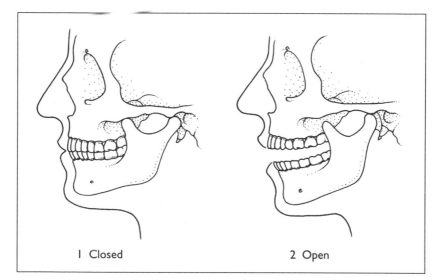

| 1 Closed | 2 Open |

The jaw in profile. Diagram 1: closed; diagram 2: open. After Bunch.

Awareness exercise 1: HOW THE JAW WORKS

Look at Diagrams 1 and 2 showing the jaw in two positions. Here's how to feel the action of the jaw working:
1. Put two fingers on the face just in front of the small flap of skin in front of each ear.
2. You can feel the head of the mandible here. Slowly open your mouth.
3. Notice how the joint moves: gliding forwards, forwards and down, and rotating as you open your mouth. This complex action is subtle in sensation. Take a few moments to repeat the action, using a mirror for visual feedback if desired.

4. Now see if you can activate some of the other muscles that work the jaw by moving it:
i.   side to side;
ii. protruding (put a finger on your chin and try to push your chin forwards into it);
iii. down and back (put a finger either side on the lower back jaws and push down and back into the fingers.

These movements are performed during chewing and eating, but not all of them are appropriate in singing.

a. Movements from side to side are a sign of asymmetrical opening of the jaw. This is by no means uncommon, as in right handedness leading to stronger muscles on the right of the body. However, an asymmetry that is visible may affect your ability to resonate and to communicate psychological states authentically.
b. Protruding the jaw is a habit often associated with poor head and neck alignment. In cases of extreme forward postures, the larynx will be drawn forwards and pushed out of alignment. This will effect sound quality and vocal efficiency.
c. Pushing the jaw down and back will activate muscles that link the tongue to the hyoid bone at the top of the larynx. Inappropriate use of these muscles can lead to tension and discomfort. The larynx will also be pushed down, causing difficulties with the upper range.

Many students with a tense jaw will try to resolve the problem by forcing the jaw open. A common exercise is to insert two or even three fingers into the mouth to encourage the jaw to open further. Very few people find this comfortable, and I have never found that it releases the jaw. If you have a tense jaw, aim to let go the muscles that are used to raise and close it. Here is an exercise that will help.

Awareness exercise 2: GIVING IN TO GRAVITY WITH THE JAW

Visual monitoring is useful for this exercise, so work with a mirror.
1. As in Awareness exercise 1, place your fingers slightly forward of the small flap in front of your ears. Move the jaw slowly forward and down, giving in to gravity.
2. Still looking in the mirror, allow your jaw to hang in this position. Notice the size of the opening. You may be surprised how small it is. Almost certainly, you will not be able to get two fingers' depth into your mouth at this stage. This is what we mean when we say 'let the jaw hang'.
3. Now we are going to use negative practice. Open the jaw further. You will probably be using muscles that make up the floor of the mouth.

Put your thumb underneath your chin to feel if you are pushing down in this area. If you can feel tension under your chin it means you are pushing *against* instead of *giving into* gravity. This is what many people need to do to find 'two fingers' depth of opening. You want to avoid this.

4. Staying with negative practice, open the jaw further still until you can feel the joint retract under your fingers. (It may feel like it disappears.) The jaw itself will be opened wide and back. Some singers feel that they need to find this position for the very top of their range. This can be useful for darkening the sound of top notes. If used indiscriminately it is likely to interfere with the free upward movement of the larynx for accessing the top of the range.

Awareness exercise 3: THE HANGING JAW POSITION

This exercise is useful if you have difficulty achieving the 'hanging jaw' position; it will enable you to let go of the powerful chewing muscles so that you can release the lower jaw.

1. Put your elbows onto a table or other suitable surface. Put your thumbs underneath the cheekbones.
2. Work your way into the non-bony area between the cheekbones, jaw and mouth, and gradually increase the pressure by pushing up with your thumbs and letting them support the weight of your head as it drops down and forward. Keep your elbows on the table for further support. Work gently during this stage, as it can be painful.
3. As you do this, allow the jaw to drop open and explore how you can let go a little more in those muscles you are feeling.
4. Slowly bring your head up again, taking care to align yourself and leaving the jaw where it is.

Awareness exercise 4: MONITORING JAW MOVEMENT

The aim of this exercise is to find an efficient use of the jaw during singing, so that the jaw does not take over tasks better served by muscles such as the tongue and soft palate.

There are two ways in which you can monitor:

i. Working with a mirror, place your hands as shown in Photograph 1 overleaf. Using this method you will be able to articulate normally and still monitor your jaw use.
ii. Put a finger in your mouth as shown in Photograph 2. Your aim is to keep the finger between your teeth but not bite down on it. Obviously you will not be able to articulate all your consonants using this method, but it gives you great feedback on jaw efficiency. I tend to use this method with clients who indulge in 'big jaw' singing all the time. Choose a song you know well and that you can sing unaccompanied.

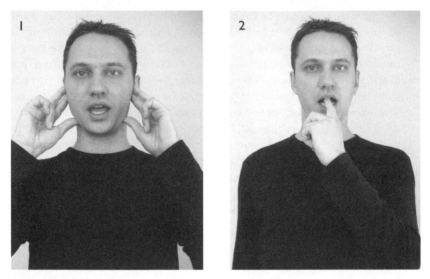

Monitoring jaw movement

1. Start by finding the hanging jaw position using Awareness exercises 2 and 3.
2. Using either of the monitoring strategies suggested above, sing the song through.
3. Notice how much or how little you are 'using your jaw' to sing the song.
4. Find out how little you can do with the jaw while still singing the song. Notice that you are now working more inside the mouth, rather than putting the work outside by using the jaw.
5. Did the song feel easier to sing with the jaw in the more efficient position?

Auditory feedback:
Repeat the exercise with a partner.
i. Sing the song without the monitoring, using your jaw in your habitual way.
ii. Using the monitoring strategies, sing the song again. Let your partner give you feedback on how the sound changed.
iii. Did you sing more loudly when you opened the jaw wider? What other effects did the change in jaw positioning have?

It is common for people to be surprised how 'easy' singing feels once they have found the comfortable jaw position for them. This is a key point. You need to find *what works for you*. Although we have the same body parts, we do not have the same dimensions. If you have a small mouth space you will not be able to move your jaw as far down as someone with a bigger frame. If your tongue is short or if you have a short tie on the underneath of the tongue (the frenulum) it is essential that you do not open the jaw too widely because your tongue will not be able to reach the hard palate for articulation. Many people who have been told that they have a problem with their jaw in fact have a problem with their tongue.

Jaw shake

Jaw shake is a distressing phenomenon for both singers and audience. In this case the jaw has become the willing slave of other muscles that are needed to support the vocal tract. Suggestions for dealing with this problem are as follows:

1. Check your general posture, paying attention to the head-neck relationship.

2. Engage the muscles that support the vocal tract from behind and at the sides.

3. With your finger in your mouth, siren your song. Aim for a sense of effort behind the nose and above the soft palate, rather than at the front of the vocal tract.

4. Miren the song (see Chapter 6 page 67), keeping the finger in place.

5. Sing the words, keeping the finger in place. Focus your effort on the muscles that anchor the vocal tract.

6. Check your airflow. Excessive airflow can destabilise the vocal tract during singing. Reduce your airflow and see if this helps.

THE TONGUE

It is not uncommon to encounter singers and teachers of my generation who were trained to keep the tongue flat with the aid of a spatula or the narrow end of a spoon. Even now I meet young singers who are trained to lower and flatten the tongue to keep it 'out of the way'.

Your tongue is big. You cannot move it out of the way. Look at Diagrams 3 and 4. There is only one place your tongue can go if you try to keep it out of the way – backwards. This will impede the space in front of the wall of the pharynx, an important resonating space, and will lead to tension at the tongue root. When we look at the tongue in a mirror, what we see is roughly two-thirds of the whole structure, usually called the tongue body or dorsum. This part of the tongue is attached loosely to the floor of the mouth via the frenulum, which you can see if you lift up your tongue. The remaining third of your tongue, called the root, cannot be

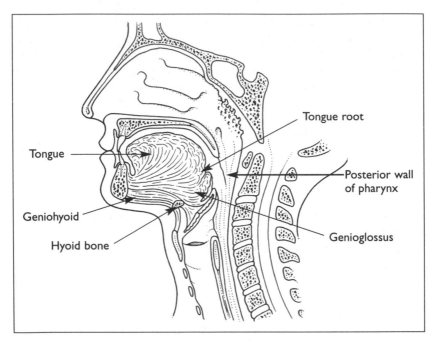

Diagram 3: Sagittal section of the head indicating the size of the tongue

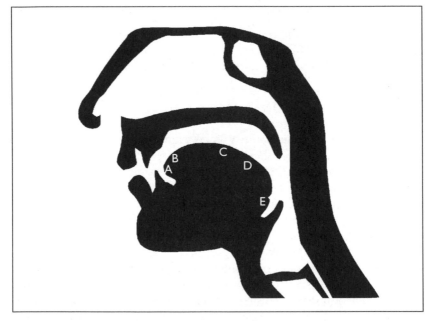

Diagram 4: Parts of the tongue. The letters indicate parts of the tongue: the tip (A), blade (B), front (C), back (D), and root (E).

seen from the front, and is attached to the hyoid bone below and to a small bone inside the skull above (styloid process). This part of the tongue is more fixed. In addition to the body and tongue root, there are numerous muscles that attach to the tongue, some of which you can see in Diagram 3.

Here are some common problems resulting from poor tongue use:

1. *Difficulty accessing the top of the range.* Your larynx needs to rise for high notes, and the soft palate muscles will tend to contract as part of this process. This means that the space for high notes is smaller.

2. *Nasality.* There are muscles attaching the back of the tongue to the soft palate. If the muscles that raise the soft palate are not firmly anchored, then lowering the tongue will pull the soft palate down, opening the nasal port.

3. *Lowering the tongue to darken the tone.* This is a technique common with Jazz and pop singers. It does darken the tone. However, depressing the tongue can lead to problems with the delicate membrane between the hyoid bone and thyroid cartilage, and it sometimes has an effect on breath use.

4. *Some vowels are heard as more resonant than others.* This is a fact of life; singers can learn to manage this so that all vowels are heard equally well.

Awareness exercise 5: THE TONGUE

1. Breathe in and out through your nose. The back of your tongue will be up against your soft palate, with the sides touching your teeth. Most of the rest of the tongue will be in contact with the roof of your mouth. This is the highest position for your tongue.
2. Yawn deeply. Notice how your tongue moves: the tip pulls back, the back of the tongue arches, and then the body of the tongue 'relaxes' on the floor of the mouth. This is the lowest position for your tongue.
3. Working with a high tongue position and then a lower one, compare the differences in sound and feel when sirening. You will find it helpful to 'think' a vowel before you start the siren. Use 'UHng' /ʌŋ/ for a low tongue and 'EEng' /iːŋ/ for a high tongue.
4. Look in a mirror, and notice what happens to the tongue when you pull your jaw down and back. Avoid pulling the tongue down with the jaw; you need a good range of movement for the tongue to shape the vowels and articulate the consonants.

The next two exercises will enable you to deal with problems **1** and **2** described above. Exercise 1 will help free up your top notes, and Exercise 2 will enable you to separate the actions of the tongue from the soft palate.

Exercise 1: THE TONGUE BACK

1. Open your mouth to the hanging jaw position (no bigger!), and extend the tongue. Push it out beyond your bottom lip (unless your tongue is really short, in which case you should adjust the exercise) and, if necessary, hold onto it with a finger.
2. So that you can get used to this position, make some noises. Remember to use the silent laugh to avoid constriction.
3. Keep the tongue extended. Starting on an easy pitch, sing an octave leap on 'AH' /ɑː/. The vowel will sound a little strange, but that doesn't matter. Notice if the tip of your tongue is pulling back as you go up in pitch; gently monitor the tongue tip with your finger to prevent this. Alternatively, you could use a mirror. If you are doing this correctly, you will notice that the back of the tongue bunches up as you slide up to the high notes. Most of your larynx is suspended from the tongue via the hyoid bone. Raising the back of the tongue will give you easier access to the high notes.
4. Work your way up through your range, bringing in any other adjustments such as anchoring or thyroid tilting as you need them. Work this exercise until you can do it without discomfort.
5. Once you have reached the top of your range, start to descend, still singing on 'AH' /ɑː/. Gradually take your finger away (or stop watching in the mirror), and withdraw the tongue to its normal positioning inside the mouth. The back of the tongue will still rise for the high notes.

Exercise 2: SEPARATING THE ACTION OF THE TONGUE AND SOFT PALATE

1. Using either of the monitoring strategies from Awareness exercise 4 on page 93, go through the palate control sequence from Chapter 6 page 61 using the vowels 'EE' /iː/ to 'OO' /uː/.
2. Remember to bring the back of the tongue and the soft palate up to meet the back wall of the pharynx as you prepare to make the consonant 'g'. Let the tongue drop as you move into the vowel.
3. You could use further monitoring by feeling the underneath of your chin with one or two thumbs. It is normal to feel some movement on 'EE' /iː/. Otherwise the movements should be small.
4. Move from 'ng' /ŋ/ to each vowel fairly slowly at first so that you have thinking and feeling time. Then increase your speed.

VOWEL FORMATION

For the work in this section you may like to use the vowel keys on pages 42–3 as a reference point. If you read phonetics you will be able to work straight from the text.

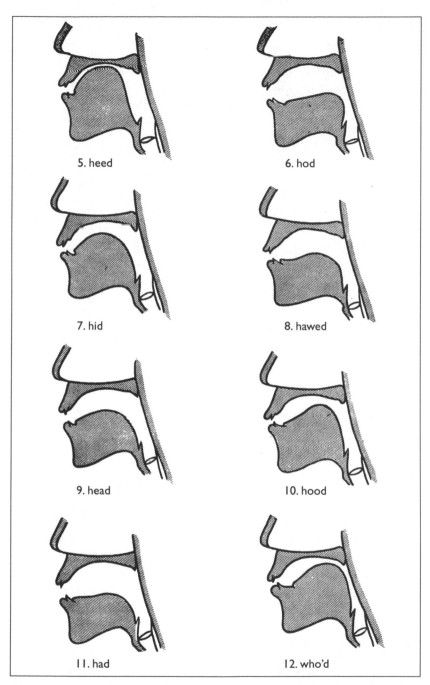

Diagrams 5–12: The positions of the vocal organs for the words 'heed', 'hod', 'hid', 'hawed', 'head', 'hood', 'had' and 'who'd' (based on X-ray photographs).

Let's consider how the vowels are formed. Look at Diagrams 5–12 of eight simple vowels (after P Ladefoged's Elements of Acoustic Phonetics, University of Chicago Press, 1962). Why do so many people have difficulty singing the vowel 'AH'? I began this chapter by commenting on this phenomenon, and now I'll answer the question. Not all vowels are made equal. It is clear from the diagrams that there is a change in the vocal tract shape for each of the vowels. This means that the resonance also changes. Each of the vowels is characterised by an identifiable patterning of harmonics, usually called vowel formants. These can be seen quite clearly on a simple spectrogram, which gives a visual representation of your sound signal. Software for voice analysis programmes can be downloaded from the Internet for free, and you might enjoy exploring some of the exercises that follow, using this type of visual feedback.[1]

The formants of the front vowels range to higher frequencies than those of the back vowels. These higher frequencies of the front vowels are more easily heard by the ear of the listener; conversely, the back vowels are less easily heard. We need to sustain pitch in singing, and we may not want a noticeable fall-off in volume from syllable to syllable. Usually singers are very conscious that some vowels are perceptually 'weaker' than others. The temptation is to distort or change the weak vowels to sound and feel the same as the 'stronger' vowels. Vowel modification needs to be a conscious choice. It is used by classical, jazz and pop singers, and not always with discrimination. An actor's task is to deliver sung text while maintaining the integrity of the vowel. This includes singing in accents or dialects. The following technique of *medialisation* will help you to achieve this.

Medialising, or tuning the vowel formants

For centuries singers have worked on equalising or matching vowels. For this reason vowel work forms a significant part of many types of vocal training. Many of the strategies used are based on the placement of Italian vowels, which are highly prized in classical singing. Another device in common use is to modify the vowels by 'covering' the brighter front vowels so that they match with the darker back and open vowels. Neither of these strategies is appropriate for musical theatre. Medialising is a solution to vowel inequality that works well for actors and musical theatre singers. Medialising means 'to make in the middle'. Specifically, it means that you are making the differences between the vowels in the middle of the tongue rather than front to back. This in turn will adjust the

---

[1] See Glossary for information about voice analysis software.

vowel formants, enabling you to equalise the vowels for resonance. Using medialising you will be more easily heard and more voice-efficient. This technique and the exercises associated with it will help you target problems 3 and 4 identified on page 97.

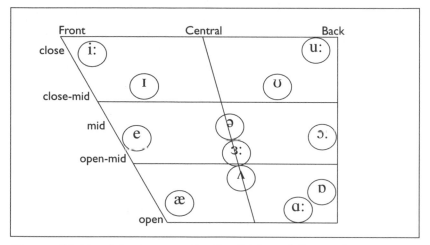

Diagram 13: Vowel chart representing the divisions of the mouth space

Look at Diagram 13. You can see that the vowels are defined according to where they are formed in the mouth space:

    i. front, central or back (and all the gradations in-between);

    ii. close, mid or open (and all the gradations in-between).

Front means near the lips and teeth, and back means near the throat. Close means near to the roof of the mouth, and open means near the floor of the mouth.

These are standard vowel placements as defined by the International Phonetic Association. Included in the box are all the simple vowels of General British speech. You might find it helpful to visualise the vowel box fitting into the mouth space as shown in Diagrams 14 and 15.

Diagram 14: 'AH' [ɑː]   *Diagram 15: medialised 'AH' [ɑː]*

Medialising involves a change of placement for the vowels. Diagrams 14 and 15 are schematic representations of two different placements for the vowel 'AH' /ɑː/. The tongue is in its most open position, lying on the floor of the mouth. In Diagram 15 you can see that there is more space between the back of the tongue and the back wall of the pharynx. This is the medialised position for 'AH' /ɑː/. The body of the tongue is raised and placed further forward in the mouth, and the tongue root is no longer covering the sound coming up from the larynx. Medialising enables you to tune the vocal tract for maximum efficiency by changing the relationship between the back of the tongue, the roof of the mouth and the back wall of the pharynx, without compromising the integrity of the vowel. It also allows for easy monitoring of tongue use by directing tongue effort onto the upper teeth. This will help you to avoid tongue backing and tongue depression.

Now look at Diagrams 16–21 opposite, which show the remaining back vowels of General British. Notice that in each medialised vowel the tongue is in a more forward position than in standard placement. The vowel box has also moved slightly forward. In medialising you are making the differences between the vowels *in the middle of the tongue*, rather than from front to back. Provided that you use the technique for all the vowels, they will be heard as authentic.

The effect of medialising is far more dramatic in the back and mid-vowels: 'OO' /uː/, 'AW' /ɔː/, 'aw' /ɒ/, 'AH' /ɑː/ and 'ER' /ɜː/. Note that the port is closed for all these vowels. Medialising the vowels need not interfere with consonant articulation.

Preparing to medialise

In General British vowel placement, the most neutral position for the tongue is the vowel of hesitation 'er' /ə/. You can see this in the middle of the vowel chart on page 101. In medialising, your starting position is from the vowel 'EE'.

Exercise 3: MEDIALISING – STAGE I

1. Raise the back of the tongue by saying 'EEng' /iːŋ /. Now spread the tongue at the back until you can feel your upper back molars with your tongue.
2. As you move through the next sounds, the back of the tongue will leave the soft palate and the body of the tongue will move forward.
3. Now say the Russian word 'nyet' /njet/.
4. Notice that the tongue rolls along the hard palate in making the 'y' /j/. Look at Diagram 15 to help you find the tongue positioning for

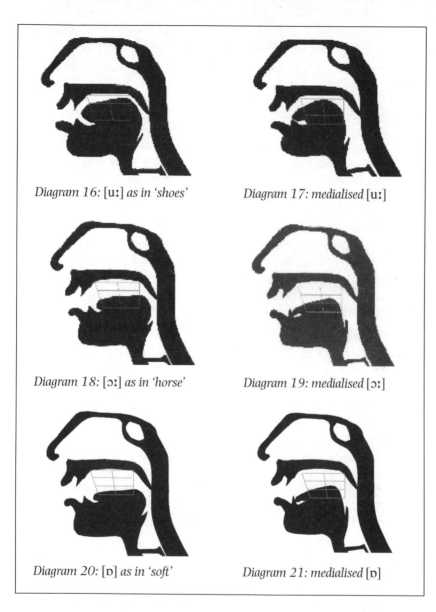

Diagram 16: [uː] as in 'shoes'

Diagram 17: medialised [uː]

Diagram 18: [ɔː] as in 'horse'

Diagram 19: medialised [ɔː]

Diagram 20: [ɒ] as in 'soft'

Diagram 21: medialised [ɒ]

medialising. The tongue needs to be positioned on the upper back molars. If your tongue cannot reach this high, make your mouth space smaller by raising the jaw a little.

5. Now say very slowly: 'nyEE' – 'nyeh' – 'nyAH' – 'nyAW' – 'nyOO' /njiː/ – /nje/– /njɑː/ – /nɔː/ – /njuː/.

General British Vowels: Monophthongs

(with lexical set in SMALL CAPS and indications of the vowel locations in **bold**)

Long Vowels

/ɑː/   open back long unrounded: as in PALM, **r**a**th**er, **m**a**rk**

/ɜː/   mid central long unrounded: as in NURSE, **b**ir**d, conf**er

/ɔː/   open-mid back long rounded: as in THOUGHT, w**a**lker, l**aw**

/iː/   close front long unrounded: as in FLEECE, m**ea**n, f**ee**d

/uː/   close back long rounded: as in GOOSE, cr**u**de, b**oo**ts

Short Vowels

/ɪ/   close-mid front short unrounded: as in KIT, st**i**ll, wick**e**d

/æ/   open front short unrounded: as in TRAP, b**a**nned, spl**a**shed

/e/   mid front short unrounded: as in DRESS, t**e**nth, s**e**ction

/ʌ/   open-mid central short unrounded: as in STRUT, w**o**rried, w**o**nders

/ɒ/   open-mid back short rounded: as in LOT, s**o**ft, c**o**stly

/ʊ/   close-mid back short rounded: as in FOOT, c**ou**ld, p**u**t

/ə/   mid central short unrounded: as in COMMA, **a**lone, m**o**th**er**

General American Vowels: Monophthongs

(lexical set in SMALL CAPS and indications of the vowel locations in **bold**)

Long Vowels

/ɑː/   open back long unrounded: as in PALM, s**o**vereign, marath**o**n

/ɝː/   rhotic mid central long unrounded: as in NURSE, **p**er**fect, ref**er

/ɔː/   open-mid back long rounded: as in THOUGHT, wr**o**ng, s**aw**

/iː/   close front long unrounded: as in FLEECE, m**ea**n, f**ee**

/uː/   close back long rounded: as in GOOSE, cr**u**de, b**oo**ts

Short vowels

/ɪ/   close-mid front short unrounded: as in KIT, st**i**ll, wick**e**d

/æ/   open front short unrounded: as in TRAP, BATH, spl**a**shed

/ɛ/   open-mid front short unrounded: as in DRESS, t**e**nth, s**e**ction

/ʌ/   open-mid central short unrounded: as in STRUT, w**a**s, wh**a**t, **u**nder

/ʊ/   close-mid back short rounded: as in FOOT, c**ou**ld, p**u**t

/ə/   mid central short unrounded: as in COMMA, th**e**, **a**lone, tak**e**n

/ɚ/   rhotic mid central short unrounded: as in LETTER, int**er**national, sug**ar**

Take time with the transition from the 'n' to the 'y' to the vowel each time, aiming to keep the sides of the tongue close to the upper back molars. Your tongue will become more concave as you move from the front to the back and open vowels.

i. Close the nasal port as you go into the vowel each time.
ii. Take a breath anytime you need it.
iii. Round your lips on 'AW' /ɔː/ and 'OO' /uː/ as usual.

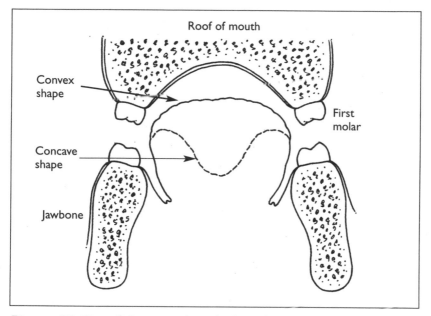

Diagram 22: View of the tongue from the front showing concave positioning

There is a significant change of positioning for the 'AH' /ɑː/ vowel, but it now matches the brightness and resonance of the 'EE' /iː/. You can equalise all the vowels for brightness using this technique. The back vowels will also feel easier to make because the sound is not being trapped between the tongue root and the pharyngeal wall.

Monitoring:
This exercise is not about fixing the tongue or pushing it upwards. Nor is it about singing with a tense jaw. These would be inappropriate tensions.

i. Using your thumb, monitor the base of the tongue by feeling for the soft part underneath your chin. As in separating the action of tongue and palate earlier in the chapter, you need only feel muscles tensing on the 'EE' /iː/ vowel.

ii. As you move from the 'n' into the 'y' /j/ you need to close the nasal port. You can check for port closure when you get to the vowel by pinching the base of the nostrils.

iii. Monitor the jaw by looking in the mirror or by feeling for the hanging jaw position described in Awareness exercise 2 on page 92.

iv. If you feel the sides of the tongue dropping away from the upper back molars during the exercise, practise moving the tongue backwards and forwards in the mouth while keeping in contact with the teeth. Find a position that works for you.

Exercise 4: MEDIALISING – STAGE 2

The aim of this exercise is to medialise the vowels without using the initial 'ny' /nj/.

1. Start in the ready position, and sing only the first vowel with the 'ny' as preparation.

'ny' – 'EE' – 'eh' – 'AH' – 'AW' – 'OO'
/nj/ – /iː/ – /e/ – /aː/ – /ɔː/ – /uː/

2. Make the changes from one vowel to the next slowly at first, and then gradually build up speed: 'nyEE' – 'eh' – 'AH' – 'AW' – 'OO' /njiːeaːɔːuː/.
3. Now do the whole sequence only on vowels using different notes in your range: 'EE' – 'eh' – 'AH' – 'AW' – 'OO' /iːeaːɔːuː/.
4. On a descending scale go through pairs of vowels on the same note, always starting with 'EE' /iː/. Work in all the simple vowels from the chart on page 42.

'EE' – 'eh'   'EE' – 'AH'   'EE' – 'AW'   'EE' – 'OO'
/iː/ – /e/   /iː/ – /aː/   /iː/ – /ɔː/   /iː/ – /uː/

You can work through your entire range in this way. You will soon find that there is no change in resonance and energy as you go from one vowel to another.

Song assignment 1: ANYONE CAN WHISTLE; YOUR SONG

Here is a typical problem area from Sondheim's '*Anyone Can Whistle*'. The extract is in the original key. Higher voices can do this exercise starting on E.

| What's | hard | is | sim - ple. | What's | na -tu -ral | comes | hard. |

There is an 'AH' /ɑː/ vowel on a high note, and you may well have difficulty with it because you are flattening and depressing the tongue.

1. Sing the top note on 'hEE' /hiː/ then 'hyAH' /hjɑː/, keeping the tongue close to the hard palate. When you do this exercise for the first time, you may find that you sing sharp on the top note. This may be because you have been compensating in some way for the loss of resonance on the 'AH' /ɑː/. Now that you can medialise the vowels, adjust your tuning accordingly, and notice that you are more voice-efficient The principle will be exactly the same if you are singing in American; the only difference will be the use of the vowel with 'r' colouring, e.g. 'urr' /ɝ/.

2. Continue doing this with any problem vowels in any song you are learning, scrolling through the vowels to the one you need to sing, making the tongue more concave for the open and back vowels as required.

THE LIPS

The lips form the front of the oral cavity and hence are the end point of the vocal tract. Several groups of muscles control the lips, and, together with the tongue, they are needed to articulate consonants and to form some of the vowels. These muscle groups fall into five categories:

1. muscles that raise the upper lip and corners of the mouth;
2. muscles that close and protrude the lips (as in kissing);
3. muscles that depress the lower lip;
4. muscles that pull back the corners of the mouth and lips;
5. muscles that protrude the lower lip (as in pouting).

Lip protrusion, or rounding, is essential for the following vowels:

1. 'OO' /uː/: the lips should be well-rounded, and the back of the tongue should be close;
2. 'ou' /ʊ/ (as in book): the lips should be slightly less rounded and more open, and the back of the tongue should be mid-close;
3. 'AW' /ɔː/: the lips should still be protruded but less rounded, and the back of the tongue open to mid;
4. 'aw' /ɒ/: the lips should be rounded but less protruded, and the back of the tongue open.

The lips are also involved in the formation of the following consonants:

1. 'p', 'b' and 'm': both lips;
2. 'f' and 'v': lips and teeth;
3. 'w': lips and velum.

Exercise 5: WORKING THE LIPS

Working in front of a mirror, perform the following facial movements. Work each stage for a few minutes at a time, alternating each new posture with a neutral, relaxed expression.

1. With the lips closed, sneer. Spread the nostrils a little, and also draw the upper lip towards the nose by shortening the space between the upper lip and nose.
2. With the lips open, insert the top of your thumb between the upper and lower teeth. Try to raise the upper lip on its own. Keep the tongue and jaw relaxed. (You can insert the thumb up to the knuckle joint providing it is comfortable for you.) This will work the muscles that raise the upper lip.
3. Close the lips and smile like the 'Joker' in *Batman*. You will be working the muscles that lift the corners of the mouth.
4. Open the mouth again to the thumb-knuckle position. Take the thumb away and make fish lips like a goldfish – alternately rounding and pulling back the lips.
5. With the jaw closed, pull your mouth down in a frown. Now stick your lower lip out as if in a sulk. This sequence works the muscles that depress the lower lip.
6. To work the muscle which links the chin to the lips, open your jaw again and try to make your chin quiver like a crying child. Your lower lip should still protrude.
7. With the jaw closed, smile; make a wide-spread smile that flattens into your face. Then smile very smugly, this time keeping the corners of your mouth in. You are now working the muscles that pull back the corners of the mouth.

Work these exercises for a few minutes at a time, alternating each new posture with a neutral, relaxed expression.

In Chapter 3, we discovered that the larynx can raise and lower, making the vocal tract tube longer or shorter. You can also adjust vocal tract length with the lips. Here's an exercise for adjusting your resonating quality using the lips.

Exercise 6: LENGTHENING THE VOCAL TRACT WITH THE LIPS

1. Sing on the vowel 'EE' /iː/ with the lips relaxed first and then protruded. Notice that the sound becomes slightly darker; if you go far enough forward in the lips, you will be singing the French vowel 'u' /y/.
2. Try this with any of the vowels that are normally made with the lips relaxed. Notice that there is quite a change in vocal colour.
3. Now do the opposite, i.e. sing on 'AH' /ɑː/ and pull the lips back. You will shorten the vocal tract a little, and the sound will become brighter.

There are schools of thought in favour of both these techniques: singing with slightly protruded lips and singing with smiling lips. You can use these features to change the sound during long held notes, changing from a brighter to a more covered tone, and vice versa.

Song assignment 2: YOUR SONG

1. Choose a song that has presented you with difficulties in the past, and target the problem areas using exercises from the chapter. Problem areas might be:
i. a difficult approach to a high note on which you have previously been pushing the tongue down;
ii. a passage that never seems to sound good in your voice. This may be a part of your vocal range that just isn't very resonant (remember that the vocal tract acts as a filter for the harmonics which are amplified in resonance: it enhances some and dampens down others). You may be able to correct this by adjusting the tongue;
iii. tensing or over-working the jaw, thereby losing resonance.
2. Remember to use monitoring devices such as fingers on the jaw, one finger in the mouth, singing with the tongue out of the mouth, touching the sides of the tongue to the teeth (to help you make the tongue concave), and working with a mirror.

Your voice is an acoustic instrument. The work in this chapter will enable you to get the best out of that instrument. By understanding how to control the soft palate, tongue, jaw and lips, you can shape your sound so that it carries easily to the listener. This gives you greater freedom to concentrate on text and meaning and so connect with the audience.

Chapter 9

Twang, the singer's formant

Chapters 6 and 8 both dealt with the management of resonance: balancing oral and nasal resonance and manipulating the tongue and jaw to enhance resonances in the oral cavity. These are not the only parts of the vocal tract where we can make adjustments to increase resonance. In this chapter we shall be doing advanced resonance work, dealing with the tube of the larynx above the vocal folds.

What voice trainers and singers call resonance is a form of sound filtering. Each part of the vocal tract (the tube of the larynx, the nose, the mouth and the pharynx) has its own resonating frequency. Harmonics that are close to the resonance frequencies of the vocal tract will get stronger, and others will be damped. The peaks of energy in these harmonics are known as 'formants'. Formants enable us to identify vowels so that, even if there is no voicing at all, you can still hear the difference between a whispered 'EE' and 'OO'. The singer's formant is based on this principle and on how the ear hears. Here is a reminder of the harmonics that come with the fundamental frequency or pitch for bass low C:

The ear canal also has its own resonating frequency. When this range of frequencies are present in a note, the ear canal resonates in sympathy with them. This is one of the secrets of effortless projection: when the ear hears twang, it comes out to meet you!

THE SINGER'S FORMANT

As discussed in Chapter 8, higher harmonics are heard more easily by the ear. This is because the resonance frequency for the ear canal is between 2,500 and 4,000 Hz. These are the harmonics that we boost when using twang. This phenomenon can increase sound levels by up to 20 decibels, which is a significant amount. Because of the advantage this gives to singers – enabling them to be heard above a full orchestra without amplification – this band of harmonics has been called the singer's formant. Singers are not the only professional voice users who employ twang: trained actors also use it to fill a big space. Drill sergeants, street hawkers and newspaper sellers use it too.

Twang in its pure form is bright and brassy. Not everybody considers it pleasant. Twang is the sound of a small baby making sure that she can be heard by her carers, or a two year old overcoming the noise of a crowded bus. It is the voice of command or irritation, yet is also a component of fine operatic singing. Twang features in both the West End and Broadway musical theatre sound and is also used in pop. It can be used as a component of your sound quality (mixing) or as a voice quality in its own right. Adding twang to your sound will enable your voice to carry in large or outdoor spaces; it also gives a good clear signal from your voice to the sound desk.

So how do we do it? Look at Diagram 1 showing a view of the larynx from behind:

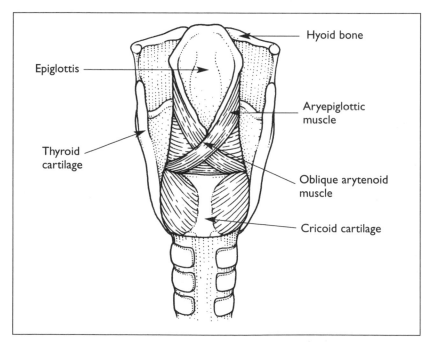

Diagram 1: View of the larynx from behind showing 'aryepiglottic sphincter'

The epiglottis and surrounding muscles are responsible for creating the extra resonance known as twang. The epiglottis is made of flexible cartilage, and it is formed in a curled leaf shape. In swallowing, the epiglottis closes over the larynx so that food and liquid can be diverted into the food pipe (oesophagus). This area is sometimes called the collar of the laryngeal tube. When muscles around the collar contract, the collar is narrowed. When this collar is narrow and the pharynx (the area outside the larynx but still inside your neck) is wide, an extra resonator is created in the vocal tract. The action of these muscles with the epiglottis is sometimes referred to as the aryepiglottic sphincter.

The aryepiglottic sphincter is narrowed by tightening muscles. It is difficult to tighten one part of the larynx without tightening another, hence falling into constriction. For this reason there are a number of conditions you need to set up before attempting twang.

Exercise 1: PREPARATION FOR TWANG

You will need to review some work from previous chapters. I will indicate which ones as we go through the preparation.
1. Check that your larynx is in a medium to high position. This is essential to finding twang. Silently siren to the top of your range, or raise the larynx by doing the first part of a swallow. We did this in Chapter 3, page 21. You may want to remind yourself of the *Isolation Checklist* to avoid undue effort.
2. Check that your tongue is also high, using the 'nyet' from Chapter 8. Monitor the tongue position by feeling for the upper back molars with the sides of the tongue.
3. Be ready to retract the false vocal folds, using the silent laugh.
4. Be ready to use thinned vocal folds as in whimpering, whining or the beginning of a siren.
5. Prepare to speak or sing with a half-open nasal port. Monitor your sound by pinching the end of the nostrils as on page 62 of Chapter 6. Make vowels with an open port 'EE', 'eh', 'AH', 'AW', 'OO' /ĩː/, /ẽ/, /ãː/, /ɔ̃ː/, /ũː/ Working twang with a half-open nasal port enables you to fool the larynx out of completing the swallow manoeuvre. This would cause you to close up the larynx and constrict.

Having completed your preparation work, move on to the following exercise.

Exercise 2: TIGHTENING THE TWANGER

Here are several different auditory cues for exploring twang. Try them all out, and then use the ones that work best for you in the exercises that follow.

1. Cackle like a witch (make sure she is a happy witch).
2. Yowl like a hungry cat.
3. Quack like an excited duck.
4. Taunt like a naughty child 'Nyea-nyea-nyea nyea-nyea'.

You might also like to use role models:

5. Imitate the speaking voice of a cartoon or television character with a shrill, piercing voice. Characters from children's programme, are often useful. (Avoid using voices that are rough or rasping as role models.)
6. Imitate the voice of Laurence Olivier saying the opening lines of Richard III: 'Now is the Winter of our discontent made glorious Summer by this sun of York.'
7. Make the sound of a discontented child nagging to go out or to stay up late.
8. Raise your voice like a mother calling her children to dinner, when they are outside or upstairs.

You may be able to find other examples that resonate with your auditory memory. Listen to the change in your sound quality when you use the above sounds. It will be bright, shrill, piercing, and will have 'edge' and 'cut'.

Kinaesthetic cues
The feeling of twang may be different from your normal voice mode:

   i. In your mouth, the space may feel horizontal rather than vertical.

   ii. The sound may feel 'buzzy' and bright inside your mouth and behind your cheekbones.

   iii. There may be a sense of effort in the soft palate and in the tongue.

   iv. It may feel as though you are making a smaller space in the larynx.

   v. It may feel as though your sound is being carried effortlessly 'away' from you.

Exercise 3: TWANGING

1. Starting with a thin fold setting and a higher laryngeal position (see 'preparation for twang'), make the sound of your choice. Use this muscle memory to guide you through the rest of the exercise.
2. Remember to monitor your tongue position, maintaining contact with the upper back molars, as before.
3. Sounds that start with a nasal consonant are favourable for twanging. As a practice sound, we are going to use 'nyeeow' /njiːɛɑːɔːuː/. This is a variant of the cat's yowl, and it will help you to keep the tongue high during twang.

4. Continue 'nyeeowing' without singing, and explore different notes in your range. Start where you can find the twang, and move up and down in pitch.

Monitoring effort:
If you feel effort at vocal fold level or a sensation of something pressing in or down in your larynx, you are making the effort in the wrong place. Here are some guidelines for checking your effort levels:

    i. Using the 'y' /j/ of the 'nyeeow', let the tongue roll forwards along the hard palate before you make the vowel. This will keep the tongue high, which is essential for twanging.

    ii. Focus your effort on the hard palate and behind the nose as you form the 'n' /n/ in preparation for twang. Avoid putting your effort into the vocal folds lower down.

    iii. Use only a little breath to make the sound, as you would for sirening or thin folds. Avoid taking a deep breath because you anticipate a loud sound.

    iv. Remember to retract the false vocal folds; twang need never feel uncomfortable.

    v. Notice changes of effort in twanging in different parts of your range. Some people will drop out of twang as they go through the gear change to the lower range; some people will tighten up too much as they approach the top of the range.

If the resultant sound is shrill and piercing inside your head, you have found your twanger. Remember that Exercise 3 is about working muscles, not beauty of sound. Allow the sound to be what it is; it can be modified later.

Sustaining pitch with twang

Once you have got the feel and sound of twang, you can start sustaining pitch. When you do this, aim to pitch a note close to that of the auditory cue of your choice. This will help you to embed the muscle memory for twang. The back and open vowels, e.g. 'OO' /uː/, 'aw' /ɒ/, 'AW' /ɔː/ and 'AH' /ɑː/, are more difficult to twang. If you have mastered the medialised position for these vowels from work in Chapter 8, you will be able to overcome this difficulty.

Exercise 4: TWANGING WITH ALL VOWELS

1. Start by twanging on one of the front vowels: 'EE' /iː/, 'eh' /e/ or 'ae'/æ/.
2. Now move from your first vowel through a sequence of five, singing 'nyEE' /njiː/ to 'nyOO' /njuː /all on one note. Keep the mouth space

small. The space inside the larynx needs to be wide, so use the silent laugh. Round your lips on the 'AW' /ɔː/ and 'OO' /uː/.

'NYEE' 'NYeh' 'NYAH' 'NYAW' 'NYOO'
/njiː/ /njeː/ /njɑː/ /njɔː/ /njuː/

3. Practise moving through the vowels by slowing down the component sounds in the cat's yowl. You can make five vowels this way:

'm – i – (e) – a – o – w'
'ny – i – (e) – a – o – w'

Monitoring effort

If you make a rasping sound or feel something scratch in the larynx, you have either constricted the false vocal folds or have pushed with the true vocal folds (pressed phonation).

   i. Use the silent laugh to release any constriction.

   ii. Siren from a higher note down towards your start note to get thinner vocal folds.

   iii. Do not drive the breath. If you push air through the twanger it will make you constrict. Use no more air than you do for the siren.

   iv. Your nasal port will still be half-open – this is OK.

For the following exercise you may find it helpful to review the work we did on smoothing out the gear changes in Chapter 5, Exercise 3 and Chapter 7, Exercises 6-9. Remember that below the first gear change the vocal folds will tend to be thicker. The larynx needs to rise for you to negotiate the gear change into the top of the range. These changes might have a knock-on effect lower down in the larynx, causing you to constrict or perhaps to lose your twang.

Exercise 5: TWANGING THROUGH THE RANGE

Here is a simple music exercise that you can use for exploring twang through the range. Sing the pattern, beginning on any note.

Below are some strategies for dealing with the potential problems:

i. *Losing the twang as you descend the scale.* This can be due to the larynx lowering. In twanging you need to have a higher laryngeal position than your norm for the low notes. Refer to Exercise 3, Chapter 3, for raising the larynx on page 21 to resolve this problem.

ii. *Problems going up into the top of the range.* Sometimes your voice will cut out, usually due to constriction. Stop and find your target note on a siren. Then put the twang back into the note. You may need to reduce the amount of twang you are using to find a comfortable effort level.

iii. *Problems with vocal fold mass.* Remember that twang is best made with thinned vocal folds. You can either maintain your thin fold setting by keeping the sensation of thyroid tilt, or you can release the tilt somewhat and allow the vocal fold mass to increase to thicker folds.

Avoid putting twang on top of vocal folds at their thickest, as this tends to lead to pressed phonation. You need to aim for a balanced effort level between the vocal folds and the tightening of the aryepiglottic area.

For a more advanced version of this exercise use a descending eight-note scale.

Exercise 6: ORAL TWANG

All of the previous exercises have been geared towards starting in nasal twang, that is, with the nasal port half-open. The aim of this exercise is to separate twang from nasality.

1. Review opening and closing the nasal port. Pay particular attention to the change of sensation from half-open to closed port (page 62).
2. Aim to separate the movement of the soft palate from the tongue by monitoring the tongue position with the sides on the upper back molars.
3. Remember that you close the port 'up' and not down.
4. Tighten the twanger as you sing very slowly: 'nyEE' /njiː/.

i. Feel your tongue roll forwards along the hard palate as you sing the 'y' /j/, and close the port as you sing 'EE' /iː/.
ii. Keep a thin fold effort level in the vocal folds (the same as for sirening).
iii. If you lower your larynx or push the back of the tongue down as you go into oral twang, you will lose the twang.
iv. Monitor your tongue positions as described in stage 2 and your larynx height with your finger as described on page 18, Chapter 3.

Almost every time I run a workshop that includes working on twang, somebody will ask: 'isn't that nasality?' Many people incorrectly identify the sound of twang as being one of 'forced' or hyper-nasality. The following exercise, which applies work from Chapter 6, enables you to feel the difference between a nasal and oral twang.

Exercise 7: NASAL TO ORAL TWANG

1. Repeat Song Assignment 3 from Chapter 6, page 69. You will remember that there are no nasal consonants in this song, so it can be done with the port closed throughout.
2. To integrate twang into the song, insert 'ny' /nj/ before each syllable, singing the correct vowels.
3. Keeping the sound and feel of the twang, repeat the song, singing the words as normal. Monitor for nasality by touching just underneath your nostrils. Since there are no nasal consonants in the song, there should be no sound coming down the nose.
4. If you find that you are falling into nasal twang, review Exercise 4 from Chapter 6 on page 62, for half-open to closed nasal port.

Problems with twang

Twang is a high intensity voice quality. Because it is made by tightening muscles in the larynx, twang needs to be avoided by the inexperienced singer or by those who are experiencing vocal problems.

1. Singers with poor vocal fold closure need to address effort levels in the breath and vocal folds before attempting twang. If your voice is habitually breathy, even when you feel you are working hard, seek the advice of a good teacher before moving on to twang.

2. Singers with pressed phonation also need to avoid twang as it may cause them to overload the vocal folds further. As a guideline, if you cannot siren well or sing softly with ease, it's not a good idea to twang until you have done some more work on your voice.

3. Singers who have twang in their habitual speaking pattern may well automatically bring twang into their singing voice. Twang is not always welcome if you are singing a soft romantic ballad or need to blend in an ensemble with other singers. If you find it difficult to switch off your twang, lower your larynx by sirening down towards the bottom of your range. Hold the lower laryngeal position, and sing the notes of your song or vocal exercise. This will help you to let go of the muscles that tighten to make twang.

You will find twang an invaluable tool in singing and speaking. You are fortunate if you already have twang in your muscular memory. Teaching in the UK I frequently work with singers to develop more twang. Working abroad in countries where twang is part of the cultural sound, I am often asked to help eliminate it. It is a matter of balance and of choice. The work in this chapter will help you to make and carry out that choice.

SECTION THREE

Working the Text

The final section of the book takes you into the realm of performance: a process for preparing a song from scratch to the advanced work of making and carrying out choices. In Chapter 10 I have suggested song extracts to work that deal with specific problems. These will help you to recognise similar trouble spots in other song material. In this section you will also be tackling the important task of delivering the text, rather than focussing on vocal production. I would expect advanced performers to make straight for this final section, starting with Chapter 11. The song exercises given in Chapter 13 are intended as guides and can be followed up with any song material that you find preferable, or need to work on.

Chapter 10

Putting it together

The aim of this chapter is to gather together the tools you have acquired so far and to put them to practical use in song learning. Many actors do not read music and so find it difficult to learn songs on their own. When learning a new song, a minimum of one session with a reliable coach is essential for those who do not read music. The session needs to include making a rehearsal recording on which the notes and rhythms are clearly indicated. Even those who do read music will benefit from a session with a singing teacher, vocal coach or pianist who can play the accompaniment stylishly and accurately. The remainder of the rehearsal process can be done independently and involves discovering what is needed to deliver the song successfully. This includes personal practice and targeting specific problem areas.

Learning sung text is more than memorising the words and melody. You need a strategy for committing words and music to your muscular memory. For the following song assignment, you need to work with someone who can take you through the notes and rhythms if you do not read music. Choose a short song that you do not know, and make sure to go through each step of the process.

Song assignment 1: YOUR SONG

1. Speak the text aloud.
Use your normal speaking voice, paying attention to stress, inflection and meaning. Some of these will change slightly when you add the melody and rhythm, but that doesn't matter at this stage.
2. Speak the text in rhythm.
    i. Using finger snapping or hand clapping, set up a steady pulse that will underlie the words all the way through and help you to count out longer and shorter beats.
    ii. Speak the text line by line in the rhythm of the music. You will find that you are intoning as opposed to singing the words as you sustain each syllable for its note value. If you do not read music, your coach should read one line at a time for you to repeat.
    iii. Scan the phrase lengths and pay attention to airflow.
    iv. Notice any difficult sounds.
    v. Notice any word or phrase stresses that have changed as a result of the set rhythms.

120

*learning lines &
learning songs not so different!*

This stage of the song learning is critical: many actors have difficulty with singing because they cannot get used to having both the rhythm and the pace of the text dictated by the music. Think of the musical structure as an extra dimension that you can use in performance, rather than as a straightjacket. Do not move on to the next stage until you are confident that you have mastered the note rhythms.

3. Siren the melody line by line.

Sirening programmes in the notes of the song, helping you embed muscle memory for pitch. If you do not read music and have no instrument to give you the actual pitch, work with someone who can play the melody for you to listen to and who can play along with you when you repeat it.

   i. As with step 2, listen to the song line by line, then siren it back. Siren quietly so that you can 'listen with the muscles'.

   ii. Work at your personal thinking speed, even if it is slower than the performance speed of the music.

   iii. Siren the melody again. This time you may work with longer sections of the music (such as four or eight bars at a time). The accompanist or instrumentalist should supply the *melody only*. It is important not to be distracted by other melodic material at this stage.

   Sirening also helps to set up your voice for singing rather than speaking. In addition, it will enable you to direct your attention towards difficult intervals between notes, and to identify gear changes in your range.

4. Miren the melody.

This step is an important interim that marries words with melody. Revise mirening from Chapter 6, page 68 Work in four to eight bar sections as appropriate.

5. Sing the words and melody of the song.

   i. Sing the whole song through with the melody only for accompaniment.

   ii. Work at your personal thinking speed. Singing is a complex task, requiring coordination between the brain hemispheres.

   iii. Have your vocal coach play or set down the full accompaniment separately so that you can listen to it before attempting to put stages 1-5 into practice against the full backing and up to speed.

This whole process takes around twenty minutes. If you record the session when you are working with a teacher or song coach, you will find it invaluable for personal practice. This process works equally well for both those who do and do not read music. Actors who use it can learn their material quickly and reliably, and they will usually have less technical difficulties with their song. Using this process I can, if necessary, prepare an actor for an audition in one session.

Gillian Kayes (Author) & so transition to from text to lyrics can't be that difficult

KNOWING WHAT AND HOW TO PRACTISE

This is probably one of the most important topics for singers in training. Clients frequently ask me how much and how often they need to practise. A more important question is '*what* do I need to practise and *how?*' Firstly, you do not need to practise something you can already do well. Other than making sure that your voice is up and running for a day's work, you generally do not need to practise a lot of vocal exercises. If you use a simple routine that involves the voiced fricatives from Chapter 4 page 30, the silent laugh routine from Chapters 2 and 5, pages 12 and 45, and the siren from Chapter 5 page 48, this will be sufficient to get your voice ready to work. When you are learning new skills you may need to spend some time practising them. Examples might include controlling pitch and range, controlling the soft palate, or learning a new vocal set up (see Chapter 12). After that, what you need is to rehearse. Rehearsal includes song-learning, decision-making (see Chapter 13), checking that you are able to articulate sung text (see Chapter 11), and troubleshooting technical difficulties within the song. The remainder of this chapter deals with this last topic. We will work through a checklist of techniques you can apply in specific situations. Two well-known songs from the musical theatre repertoire are suggested for exploration: '*I've Never Been in Love Before*' from *Guys and Dolls* by Frank Loesser, and '*If I Loved You*' from *Carousel* by Rodgers and Hammerstein. They can be sung in any key and performed by either a male or female voice. Extracts from additional song material are also given for application in specific situations.

Monitoring constriction

If you are feeling discomfort during rehearsal or your voice quality is rough and raspy you may be constricting. This can often happen when learning new material. Here are some general points to be aware of in personal practice:

1. Practise your chosen song using the siren line by line. Silently chuckle or giggle before and after each phrase. Use the 'widened thumbs' position, external monitoring or an elastic band as reminders for the silent laugh posture. (See Chapter 5 pages 46–7.)

2. You can also sing the song silently to target constriction. Put your fingers in your ears. Make sure that there is no sound inside your head. Mouth the words in time with the rhythm and pretend to sing. Make sure you are breathing out when 'singing', and allow the breath to come in between phrases. Do this for a couple of phrases in a song and then repeat, singing out loud. This will help you develop a muscle memory for the widened false vocal folds.

Range work in songs

Inexperienced singers will often hunt for songs that do not cross their 'break'. Sadly, not many of these songs exist, so you will usually have to deal with range issues at some point in the song. Both *'I've Never Been in Love Before'* and *'If I Loved You'* range through an octave and a half, and so they require you to change gear at some points. The following sequence will help you to target the gear changes in the song of your choice:

Song assignment 2: TARGETING GEAR CHANGES

1. Warm up using the siren. Find the pitch range of the song and siren octave slides to cover that range.
2. When going through a gear change, think ahead. If you can prepare your muscles ahead of time you are more likely to negotiate the change smoothly. (See Chapter 2 page 12 and Chapter 5 page 50.)
3. As a general rule, use thyroid tilt to move upwards, and thin the vocal folds. Release the thyroid tilt to move downwards for accessing the lower range. Exceptions would be when using belt voice quality.
4. Remember that you may need to use vocal tract anchoring to support your voice during the gear change. (See Chapter 7 page 85.)
5. As a general rule, when accessing the top of your range, remember to keep the nasal port firmly closed, enabling the muscles that raise the larynx to do their work. Practise singing 'ngGEE' on notes that are giving you problems. Then move into the written vowel, starting with 'ng'.
6. Monitor your tongue and jaw use during gear changes. Notice if you pull the jaw down and/or flatten the tongue when approaching your high notes. Use the 'finger in mouth' or 'hands on the jaw joint' strategies as described in Chapter 8 page 93.
7. Singing with the tongue extended and gently held with one finger can be helpful for accessing top notes that you know are in your range. Avoid pulling the tongue down and back, away from your finger. (See Chapter 8 page 98.)

Song assignment 3: MANAGING SUDDEN LEAPS IN THE RANGE WITH 'ANYONE CAN WHISTLE'

Sudden leaps can present a challenge, leading to difficulties with pitching or with changing gear. It is easier to manage them in the range by silently preparing the muscles for the pitch.

Look at the extract from Stephen Sondheim's *'Anyone Can Whistle'*.

It's   all   so   sim - ple: Re - lax,   let   go,   let   fly,

1. Begin by sirening between the first two notes of the phrase ('It's all') so that you can get a muscular 'feel' for the interval of a 7th. Do this several times if needed.
2. Sing the first note out loud and then siren up to the second note. Do this at thinking speed; you do not need to sing the correct note values to begin with.
3. Sing the first note out loud and prepare the pitch for the second note by silent sirening up to it.
4. Sing the whole phrase using the correct note values.
   This strategy works equally well for downward drops in pitch.

Breath management

Breath management needs to be tailored to the needs of the song. This includes considerations such as choice of voice quality, musical style and other interpretive issues. We shall be covering these in the final chapters of the book. This section will enable you to target a number of common breathing difficulties: insufficient airflow, locking the in-breath, breathy tone and over-breathing.

Song assignment 4: TARGETING INSUFFICIENT AIRFLOW AND LOCKING WITH 'I'VE NEVER BEEN IN LOVE BEFORE'

1. Sing the melody on voiced fricatives such as 'v' /v/ or 'z' /z/. Make sure that you are moving the centre of the belly towards the backbone when you make the sound and that you are able to recoil at the ends of phrases. Use the diamond of support (page 34) if you need more sustaining power. You can monitor the four points of the diamond with your hands.
2. If you feel that you are locking the breath at the ends of phrases, try rubbing your belly with both hands while singing. This will help you to get in touch with the sensation of elastic recoil.
3. Remember that you use more breath when singing on voiced fricatives than you are likely to need in the song. To balance your airflow, alternate voiced fricatives and words, phrase by phrase.
4. Remember that you do not need to use up all your air each time you sing a phrase. Whenever you want to breathe, simply let go of the abdominal wall.

Song assignment 5: TARGETING BREATHY TONE WITH 'I'VE NEVER BEEN IN LOVE BEFORE'

Breathy tone is generally a result of too little resistance at vocal fold level. This can sometimes be remedied by using voiced fricatives (as in Song assignment 4, stage 3), but not always.

1. Insert a glottal onset each time you sing 'I' to set up a higher level of resistance in the vocal folds. If you continue on to the end of the song ('in love before'), remember to use vocal tract and torso anchoring to support this more energised voice use (see Chapter 7 pages 77 and 81).
2. Once you have established the increased vocal fold mass, you can smoothe out the glottal onsets if you wish.
3. Twang is sometimes helpful in addressing a breathy voice. Practise each note of the song using 'nyeeow' to work twang. Then sing the words.

Over-breathing is a very common problem that results from a mistaken idea that both airflow and breath pressure are constant in singing. This is not the case. Subglottic pressure (the air held back by the vocal folds) varies according to the dynamic level (loud or soft), the pitch (less breath for high notes, more for low notes) and from syllable to syllable (the breath flow will stop for stopped consonants and increase for fricatives). Excessive vibrato may also be a by-product of over-breathing.

Song assignment 6: TARGETING OVER-BREATHING WITH 'I'VE NEVER BEEN IN LOVE BEFORE'

1. Sing the song first on a siren and then on a miren. Notice how little breath is required.
2. Sing the song on vowels only, using first one vowel, then the vowels for each syllable. Your breath use will be relatively smooth and uninterrupted within each phrase.
3. Notice what happens when you go up in range: you will tend to use less breath and work more in the postural anchoring muscles.
4. Now add the words. Notice that the airflow is different because you have introduced consonants. This will be particularly noticeable when you sing words that have stopped consonants or fricatives, e.g. 'before', 'at', 'once' and 'it's'.
   In speech the rapid changes of airflow between voiceless and voiced sounds are generally unproblematic. In sustaining pitch, the task becomes more complex, and constriction can occur if you are unable to coordinate pitching with these changes.
5. Practise singing the words 'but this is wine' and 'that's all too strange and strong' on one note, focusing on what is happening as you move from the vowels to the consonants. (Look at the music example on page 126.) Sometimes the breath will be stopped altogether; sometimes you will need more breath to make the consonant. You might like to monitor your abdominal wall during this exercise to find out how flexible you need to be with your breath use when singing words.

6. Now sing the phrases worked on in stage 5 on the written notes. You may find that your breath use is more efficient because you have worked out how to manage your breath appropriately for the task of sung text.

Additional problems in breath management might be a lack of sustaining power or excessive vibrato in the production (wobble). The following song assignment uses strategies from Chapter 4.

Song assignment 7: TARGETING LACK OF SUSTAINING POWER WITH 'I'VE NEVER BEEN IN LOVE BEFORE'

For this song, as in many classic book musicals, 'legit' singing is required. You will need to sing the first phrase in one breath, with a full and lyrical tone.

1. Sing the first phrase on the rolled 'R' or lip trill. Put your hands around the waistband (see Chapter 4, pages 31–2) so that you can feel its lateral movement.
2. When you want to breathe in, release the waistband. You should re-engage it as you start to sing the next phrase on the rolled 'R' or lip trill. If you are performing the elastic recoil correctly and engaging the waistband, you will quickly build enough sustaining power to sing each of the first four phrases, one after the other. (Breathe in after the words 'before', 'safe', and 'score'.)

   Some Musical Directors will ask you to sing the following phrase in one breath. You may find this a challenge.

3. Continue working with the rolled 'R' or lip trill. As you sing the note for the word 'wine', which is three beats long, consciously engage the waistband on the long note, and you will make it to the end of the phrase.

Song assignment 8: TARGETING EXCESSIVE VIBRATO WITH YOUR SONG

Over-breathing can sometimes result in excessive vibrato (wobble). You can remedy this by reducing your airflow and increasing work in the anchoring muscles.

1. Using work from Chapter 7 (pages 77 and 79) work the vocal tract anchoring exercise silently.
2. Silently mouth the words of your chosen song, keeping the anchoring muscles engaged. Make sure that you are able to breathe out at this stage as in the exercise for releasing constriction earlier.
3. Siren the melody, engaging the anchoring muscles.
4. Sing the words and melody, using the same effort level in the anchoring muscles as before.

Projection and dynamic control

Remember that in order to increase volume you may need to change your setting in the vocal folds. The *messa di voce* exercise from Chapter 7 page 84 is useful for increasing and decreasing volume.

As with breath management, the degree of anchoring required depends on the vocal task. Typical situations that require anchoring are: negotiating the gear changes, long or held notes, high notes, sustained passages of music, and when your voice needs more 'presence'. The assignments that follow are on '*If I Loved You*' by Rodgers and Hammerstein. This can be a challenging song for many people because it needs to be sung reflectively and expressively, and it also demands good dynamic control.

Song assignment 9: ADDING THE VOICE-BODY CONNECTION WITH 'IF I LOVED YOU'

Here's how to stabilise your voice while finding a bigger sound:

1. Sing the song phrase by phrase. Elongate the first note of each phrase, firstly singing it 'relaxed' and then with the anchoring muscles engaged. Notice the difference in feel and sound. Continue with the rest of the phrase, holding the effort of anchoring throughout. Use the *Isolation Checklist* (page 76) to monitor for extraneous tensions.
2. Apply the same principles in anchoring the torso. Remember that, if you have a big voice, you will benefit from a degree of torso anchoring all the time. Otherwise, use the torso anchoring as you need it.
3. The anchoring muscles will tend come into play more automatically once you have rehearsed the song a few times.

Song assignment 10: CHANGING VOCAL FOLD MASS WITH 'IF I LOVED YOU'

Working with your vocal fold mass will help you control dynamic levels within a song and to be in control of your general level of projection.

1. To build volume, increase vocal fold mass and breath pressure. Use the first part of the *messa di voce* exercise from Chapter 7 page 84.
2. Practise the *messa di voce* on single notes that cover the range of your song, and then apply them to sections where you require a bigger tone.
3. Remember that the harder you are working with your vocal folds, the more you must retract the false vocal folds. Use the silent laugh.
4. When applying the *messa di voce* exercise, notice that your voice will feel more stable if you use vocal tract anchoring as you increase volume. Your tonal quality will also improve.

5. Look at the music extract above. It is usual to *crescendo* (increase in volume) at this point in the song:
i. Aim to increase volume between the first and second 'never' and then again on 'know'.
ii. Since 'know' is set on a long note, you can apply the *messa di voce* here to increase volume gradually.
iii. Hold this dynamic level for the beginning of the next phrase ('How I').

6. Consider the second music extract. At this point a *decrescendo* (decrease in volume) is indicated in the music, and it is also implied by the subtext:
i. To decrease volume, you will need to thin your vocal fold mass and decrease breath pressure. Use the second part of the messa di voce exercise to achieve this in the song.
ii. Remember that your voice will be more stable when decreasing volume if you maintain some vocal tract anchoring. This is especially important at this point since it is also contains the highest note of the song.

Note that the raised vocal fold plane position is not a good base for increasing and decreasing volume.

Song assignment 11: PROJECTION VIA THE SINGER'S FORMANT WITH YOUR SONG

This is a strategy that may be used instead of increasing vocal fold mass or anchoring, though advanced work could include all three factors.

1. To incorporate twang into your song, sing every note on 'nyeeow' /njiːeɑːɔːuː/ or 'nyae' /njæ/.
2. Speak the words of the song in a really irritating, twangy voice. It is helpful to do this on a higher pitch than your normal speaking voice; however, aim to speak close to the pitches of the song.
3. You may need to speak with a thin whining voice first to reach these pitches (speaking with thin folds). An easy way to access this is via the auditory cue of a small child calling 'mummy'.
4. To add the twang, let the childish voice become more petulant and whinging.
5. Now sing the song with the words, adding twang as desired to increase volume and excitement.

If you progress to the advanced work of twanging with a thicker vocal fold mass, balance your effort levels using anchoring and retraction and remember to go through the *Isolation Checklist*.

Using twang as a 'mix'

Twang can also be used to boost volume in parts of your range that may not be very resonant.

'Mixing' refers to any strategy a singer might use to minimise either the timbral or volume differences between the vocal registers. Traditionally classical singing training concentrates on blending or mixing head and chest registers to give the sound and feel of a whole across the range. One way or another all singers seem to use mixing, whether they are aware of it or not. This is because the voice is an imperfect instrument acoustically, so there will tend to be notes in your range that simply are not as strong in resonance as others. The two song assignments that follow are examples of situations where you can use twang as a mixer. These songs are written originally for a mezzo-soprano and tenor respectively. There is nothing to stop you working them in a key that is suitable for your voice; the principles remain the same.

Song assignment 12: THE OPENING PHRASE OF 'WITH EVERY BREATH I TAKE' BY CY COLEMAN AND DAVID ZIPPEL

Sing the opening phrase: 'There's not a morning that I open up my eyes'. The first vowel in 'morning' is a back vowel and is to be sung on a low note, which makes it doubly difficult to make the note 'speak'.

1. Sing, 'There's not a 'nyEE'–'nyEE' that I open ...'
2. Then sing, 'There's not a 'nyor-nyi-ng' that I open ...'
3. Finally, sing the words as written, working to keep your twanger tightened. You will almost certainly get a better bottom note.

Song assignment 13: THE BRIDGE PASSAGE OF 'EMPTY CHAIRS AT EMPTY TABLES' BY SCHÖNBERG AND BOUBLIL

Work on the phrase 'From the table in the corner'. This is usually sung by a tenor, who needs to make a crescendo on a phrase containing low A, often the bottom note in his range.
1. Do not lower the larynx at this point; it will only make your voice quieter and you will not be able to make the crescendo needed to indicate the rising excitement in this passage. Raise the larynx before you even start the phrase. (You are now applying work from Chapter 3.)
2. Tighten the twanger.
3. Sing 'nyom-nye nyable nyin', and so on up to 'corner', keeping the back of the tongue high. You will find that the notes speak better. If you add some anchoring as the phrase continues you will be able to make a good crescendo without straining.

Balancing resonance

There are three considerations when balancing resonance: the nasal port, the jaw, and vowel medialisation. Here you will be applying work from Chapters 6 and 8. A short song extract is suggested for practice with each of the techniques described.

The nasal port
The soft palate acts as a doorway between the nose and the mouth. The door needs to be closed if you want to form the vowels correctly and if you want a brighter resonance. The door needs to be open when you make the nasal consonants 'n' /n/, 'ng' /ŋ/ and 'm' /m/. Here are some pointers to be aware of during personal practice:
   1. Monitor the nasal port by doing the nose test (see Chapter 6, page 64). Sing phrases of songs, extracting the vowels only.
   2. Hold your nose to check that the nasal port is closed on the vowels (see Chapter 6, page 69).
   3. On the nasal consonants open the port by consciously directing the und into the nose (see Chapter 6, page 59). If you cannot feel this king, breathe out through your nose with your lips closed.
      Make the required consonant and open your mouth for 'ng' and 'n', ining the open port feel.

Song assignment 14: 'AUTUMN' FROM STARTING HERE, STARTING NOW BY MALTBY AND SHIRE (1)

Sing this short extract:

Au - tumn___

1. Ensure your nasal port is opened when you sing the final 'm' at the end of the word. Do the nose pinch to check.
2. Nasal consonants are not easily heard; make the 'm' strong enough to feel vibrations in the nose.

This song is a useful exercise because the word 'autumn' is repeated over and again.

If you work on the whole song, notice when the nasal port needs to close again for moving into vowels and non-nasal consonants.

The jaw
Sometimes people seem to be singing from their jaw. Remember that the jaw is connected to other important structures and can have a knock-on effect on them. Here is a reminder of techniques you can apply during personal practice:

1. Sing with a finger in your mouth, looking in a mirror or monitoring the joint of the jaw.

2. Aim to sing in the 'hanging jaw' position, singing first on 'EE' /iː/ and then on the vowels of song.

3. Notice if your habit is to lower the jaw for high notes. Generally speaking this will tend to depress the larynx and the tongue, which may not be helpful.

4. Sing the words of a song with the vowels and consonants, aiming to keep a comfortable jaw position.

Vowel medialisation
Remember that the purpose of medialising the vowels is to find a balanced resonance between them. Here are some techniques you can apply during personal practice:

1. Use 'nyet' /njet/ (see Chapter 8, page 102) to find the sensation of a concave tongue for the flat and back vowels.

2. Say the words of a song in rhythm, elongating any vowels on long notes.

3. Say the words of the song, medialising the vowels, checking in the mirror if you need to.

4. Remember that you can monitor your tongue position by feeling for the upper back molars with the sides of the tongue.

5. Sing the words of the song on single notes, medialising the vowels.

6. Target difficult words by starting the word on the written pitch with an 'EE' /iː/, and then moving into the written vowel or syllable.

Song assignment 15: 'AUTUMN' FROM STARTING HERE, STARTING NOW BY MALTBY AND SHIRE **(2)**

Sing this extract from the bridge section:

re - call

The music becomes more intense and the melody rises. The highest note in the song (E flat) is on the vowel 'AW' /ɔː/ (or /ɑː/ in General American) for which your tongue is at its lowest in normal vowel placement. This low tongue position can make it difficult to access the high note, which for many people will also be around their second gear change. Medialising the vowel will help you address this without losing the integrity of the vowel.

1. Sing the high note to 'EE' /iː/.
2. Sing the word again, this time moving from 'rEE'-'kEE' /rikiː/ to 'rEE'-'kAW' /rikɔː/ and finally inserting the dark 'l' /ɫ/.
3. Remember to monitor your tongue position on the upper back molars. You will be making the 'AW' /ɔː/ with a more concave tongue.

Making the tube longer and shorter
Changing the length of the vocal tract tube is a further way of altering your resonating quality. While it is not a substitute for vowel medialisation, it can have the effect of deepening your tonal quality (lengthening the tube) or brightening it (shortening the tube).

When using this strategy remember to balance considerations of resonance with those of comfortable effort levels: higher larynx for the top notes, lower larynx for the bottom notes, and neutral or rest position when no adjustment is required. Here is a reminder of techniques you can apply in personal practice:

1. *Lowering the larynx.*

i. Using the yawn-sigh manoeuvre from Chapter 3, page 21, lower your larynx.

ii. To take this a stage further, breathe out as if sobbing deeply and silently. Do it for a few moments, keeping the larynx low, even on the in-breath.

iii. Sing a song extract with your larynx in this lowered posture. Notice that it takes considerable effort to hold the larynx in this low position. This produces a more covered and dark tone.

2. *Raising the larynx.*

i. Silently siren to the top of your range, and hold the larynx in this position.

ii. Alternatively, start to swallow and stop at the point of raising the larynx. (See Chapter 3, page 22). Monitor constriction of the false vocal folds using the silent laugh.

iii. Repeat your chosen song extract in the same key with your larynx in this high posture.

In raising the larynx, it may well feel as though you are singing from a smaller space (which you are), but you will find the top notes are accessed more easily this way. Remember that it is the smaller musical instruments that are higher in range. Your own vocal instrument is immensely flexible and can change length.

Remember that raising and lowering the larynx is a matter of degree. It is neither necessary nor desirable to fix the larynx in any one position. In Chapter 12 we will consider further the height of the larynx for different vocal qualities.

Every song is a new challenge, technically and interpretively. You will find it useful to refer to the five topics under 'knowing what and how to practice' (see page 122) as a checklist when learning new song material. As you become more experienced you will start to apply these principles without being conscious of it. Remember that there is a solution to every trouble spot; it is simply a question of working out what the problem is. Essentially, that is the purpose of practising.

Chapter 11

Singing the text

Over many years of vocal training I have found that, often, vocal challenges are not about the voice but about the management of sung text. As an actor who sings you have a responsibility to ensure that your words are intelligible to the audience, even when you are singing a ballad. Sung text requires careful handing because it is easy to lose words or meaning when sustained pitch and a defined rhythmic structure are called for by the music. By focussing on the mechanics of forming the vowels and consonants you will become more involved with your text and story.

Singing is characterised by sustained pitch. Pitch and the melodic line are carried largely by vowels, which travel unobstructed through the vocal tract. This is undoubtedly why many vocal training exercises are vowel based. Consonants are defined as obstructing the vocal tract. These obstructions may be complete or partial. Specific issues arise with different types of consonant. In this chapter we shall be focusing on some of the requirements of sung text, including further work on vowels, work on consonants, style and meaning. In Chapter 13 there will be detailed work on text as journey for the audience and singer.

MAKING SENSE OF SUNG TEXT

Music has a vital role to play in sung text by enabling the audience to process information on several levels. The rhythmic, melodic and orchestral settings all contribute to this process. The actor's job is to deliver the text within this structure, not only ensuring that he or she sounds realistic, but also to ensure that the audience is able to hear the text. This may not be as easy as it sounds, since it is not just a question of volume. Put simply, it is easier to sustain pitch and to be audible on vowels than it is on consonants. The result is that consonants do not compete well with vowels in terms of audibility in singing. It is essential, therefore, that the singing actor finds ways of balancing the vowel-consonant relationship so that the text can be intelligible to the audience. In the work that follows we shall be looking at some common problems in delivering sung text, and their solutions.

Vowel integrity

Aim to sing as you would speak in the world of the character. You may also want to research any dialect or accent implied by the environment of the character, including implications of status and any historical setting. A role in Rodgers and Hammerstein's *Carousel*, for example, would call for a New England accent. A high status character, such as the Judge in Stephen Sondheim's *Sweeney Todd*, would be unlikely to speak in a regional accent, whereas Sweeney himself might well do so. All of these need to be factored in when preparing a role.

Traditional 'bel canto' training uses Italian vowels as a basis for vocal production because of their resonance properties. These vowels are rarely appropriate in musical theatre repertoire, which is mostly written in English, American English, and accents and dialects related to these. A 'bel canto' based training would be one reason why a singer might change or modify vowels in singing. A second reason would be for ease of vocal production (some vowels may feel easier to produce in certain parts of the range than others). A third would be the result of an idea about how vowels should be sung in relation to the written note values. In traditional classical and choral training, singers are usually advised to sustain the vowel for the full note value and to put the consonant before or after the note. However, this vowel-consonant relationship does not have to be fixed.

Look at the vowel chart on pages 42 and 43. There are twenty vowels in Standard British and American. Of these twenty, twelve are simple vowels (monophthongs) and eight are compound (diphthongs and triphthongs). The simple vowels include both short and long vowels. Medialising will enable you to sing any vowel, long or short, with clarity, without altering the colour of the language, and without compromising your vocal production. It can be applied to any of the English languages, and I have also used it successfully in Japanese, Spanish and German.

1. Simple vowels

Below are three examples of situations in which an actor might change the vowels in sung text. All of them arise from the way the text is set, and all are easy to address.

Begin by revising the technique of medialising the vowels, singing first on 'nyet' /njet/ and then on 'nyEE' – 'nyeh' – 'nyAH' – 'nyAW' – 'nyOO' /njiː/ – /nje/– /njɑː/ – /njɔː/ – /njuː/ (See Chapter 8, page 102).

1. Sing the first phrase of '*If I loved You*' from Rodgers and Hammerstein's *Carousel*. Focus on how you form the vowel in the word 'love'. The vowel is 'UH' /ʌ/, a mid-vowel. Using the technique of medialising, practise singing the note on 'nyEE' – 'nyeh' – 'nyUH' /njiː/ – /nje/ – /njʌ/. This will help you to get a resonant sound on the

General British Vowels: Monophthongs

(with lexical set in SMALL CAPS and indications of the vowel locations in **bold**)

Long Vowels
/ɑː/   open back long unrounded: as in PALM, r**a**ther, m**a**rk
/ɜː/   mid central long unrounded: as in NURSE, b**i**rd, conf**er**
/ɔː/   open-mid back long rounded: as in THOUGHT, w**a**lker, l**a**w
/iː/   close front long unrounded: as in FLEECE, m**ea**n, f**ee**d
/uː/   close back long rounded: as in GOOSE, cr**u**de, b**oo**ts

Short Vowels
/ɪ/   close-mid front short unrounded: as in KIT, st**i**ll, wick**e**d
/æ/   open front short unrounded: as in TRAP, b**a**nned, spl**a**shed
/e/   mid front short unrounded: as in DRESS, t**e**nth, s**e**ction
/ʌ/   open-mid central short unrounded: as in STRUT, w**o**rried, w**o**nders
/ɒ/   open-mid back short rounded: as in LOT, s**o**ft, c**o**stly
/ʊ/   close-mid back short rounded: as in FOOT, c**ou**ld, p**u**t
/ə/   mid central short unrounded: as in COMMA, **a**lone, moth**er**

General American Vowels: Monophthongs

(lexical set in SMALL CAPS and indications of the vowel locations in **bold**)

Long Vowels
/ɑː/   open back long unrounded: as in PALM, s**o**vereign, marath**o**n
/ɝː/   rhotic mid central long unrounded: as in NURSE, p**er**fect, ref**er**
/ɔː/   open-mid back long rounded: as in THOUGHT, wr**o**ng, s**a**w
/iː/   close front long unrounded: as in FLEECE, m**ea**n, f**ee**
/uː/   close back long rounded: as in GOOSE, cr**u**de, b**oo**ts

Short vowels
/ɪ/   close-mid front short unrounded: as in KIT, st**i**ll, wick**e**d
/æ/   open front short unrounded: as in TRAP, BATH, spl**a**shed
/ɛ/   open-mid front short unrounded: as in DRESS, t**e**nth, s**e**ction
/ʌ/   open-mid central short unrounded: as in STRUT, w**a**s, wh**a**t, **u**nder
/ʊ/   close-mid back short rounded: as in FOOT, c**ou**ld, p**u**t
/ə/   mid central short unrounded: as in COMMA, th**e**, **a**lone, tak**e**n
/ɚ/   rhotic mid central short unrounded: as in LETTER, int**er**national, sug**ar**

General British Vowels: Diphthongs

Centring
/ɪə/   as in NEAR, w**ei**rd, r**ea**r
/eə/   as in SQUARE, h**air**, f**air**
*/ʊə/ as in CURE, p**oor**, l**ure**

Closing
/eɪ/   as in FACE, s**ay**, aw**ay**
/aɪ/   as in PRICE, t**i**me, compl**y**
/ɔɪ/   as in CHOICE, andr**oi**d, pl**oy**
/əʊ/   as in GOAT, s**ew**, ag**o**
/aʊ/   as in MOUTH, all**ow**, v**ow**

General British Vowels: Triphthongs

/eɪə/   as in pl**ayer**, conv**eyor**, sl**ayer**
/aɪə/   as in sc**ie**nce, vi**ol**et, f**ire**
/ɔɪə/   as in l**awyer**, r**oyal**, t**oil**
/əʊə/   as in l**ower**, m**ower**, bl**ower**
/aʊə/   as in p**ower**, s**our**, fl**ower**

General American Vowels: Diphthongs

Centring
/ɪɚ/   as in NEAR, w**ei**rd, app**ear**
/ɛɚ/   as in SQUARE, d**are**, f**air**
/ɑɚ/   as in START, s**ar**dine, t**ar**
/ɔɚ/   as in FORCE, **Or**pheus, p**ore**
/ʊɚ/   as in CURE, end**ure**, cont**our**

Closing
/eɪ/   as in FACE, s**ay**, aw**ay**
/aɪ/   as in PRICE, t**i**me, compl**y**
/ɔɪ/   as in CHOICE, andr**oi**d, pl**oy**
/oʊ/   as in GOAT, v**o**gue, fell**ow**
/aʊ/   as in MOUTH, l**ou**d, v**ow**

General American Vowels: Triphthongs

/eɪɚ/   as in pl**ayer**, conv**eyor**, sl**ayer**
/aɪɚ/   as in d**ire**, adm**ire**, f**ire**
/ɔɪɚ/   as in l**awyer**, f**oyer**, empl**oyer**
/oʊɚ/   as in l**ower**, m**ower**, bl**ower**
/aʊɚ/   as in p**ower**, s**our**, fl**ower**

*often grouped with and pronounced like the THOUGHT vowel /ɔː/ in modern General British

If   I   loved you.

vowel without resorting to singing 'lAHv' /lɑːv/, or 'lawv' /lɒv/, which are commonly heard in this situation.

2. Some singers experience difficulty singing high notes on the close vowels 'EE' /iː/ and 'OO' /uː/. Here are two song extracts from '*A Call from the Vatican*' from *Nine* by Maury Yeston and '*Music of the Night*' from *Phantom of the Opera* by Andrew Lloyd Webber, Charles Hart and Richard Stilgo. These extracts can be transposed down a third if desired for lower voices.

Gui - do   be

i. Make sure you can access the pitch comfortably on a siren, putting into place technical details such as thinning the vocal folds and raising the larynx. (This works for both extracts.)

ii. Check that you are in 'hanging jaw' position.

iii. Using medialising, sing the note on first 'nye' /nje/ and then 'nyEE' /njiː/. In this case, the middle of your tongue will actually be lower than the norm for singing on 'EE' /iː/, with the more concave positioning giving you more room to sing the high note.

iv. Sing the written words.

3. In Stephen Sondheim's '*Send in the Clowns*', the word 'rich' is set on the longest note of the opening phrase. The potential problem here is that 'i' /ɪ/ is a short vowel and that the note is a long one.

rich   [riːʃ]

[r ɪ —— ʃ]

i. Think of the whole of the word being allotted to the note value, rather than just the vowel.

ii. Allot at least one beat to the 'ch' /ʧ/. This is a common practice in musical theatre style and will enable you to avoid elongating the vowel into 'reach' /riːʧ/, simply because it is set on a long note.

iii. In circumstances where there is an even longer note value (such as four or more beats) you could consider cutting the note short.

2. Compound Vowels

A few years ago I gave a series of lessons to an excellent choral conductor who wanted to learn how to use his own voice better in order to benefit his choral groups. I had also been working as a vocal coach with two of his choirs. The first edition of *Singing and The Actor* had already been published, and in due course we had a conversation about diction. My colleague was somewhat shocked at the idea of singing the diphthongs, let alone the consonants, since it went against English Cathedral choral training. However, I explained my position, and he duly went away and tried out what we had discussed with his choir. Some eighteen months later, I attended the final round of a major choral competition in the UK in which one of his young choirs was competing. Their diction was impeccable, enabling both the singers and the audience to connect to the emotional content of the material. The choir came first in its category that year. While this is a story about ensemble singing, the same holds true for solo work.

Compound vowels can present a challenge in sung text, but they are part of the English language. Learning how to manage them needs to be part of vocal training for those who want to sing in English. Largely it is a matter of timing. Here are some guidelines:

1. You will find it useful to practise speaking the words of songs out loud before singing them.

2. In English, the written form sometimes has a sketchy resemblance to the phonetic form. If you are not sure of the component sounds (phonemes) in a word, refer to the vowel key on page 42.

3. Include all the sounds in compound vowels. Remember that the transition between two sounds in a diphthong is an important cue for the audience in processing the text.

4. An exception in General British speech may be made for triphthongs (for example, 'lawyer' /lɔɪə/ and 'power' /paʊə/). It is now considered acceptable to turn the three sounds into two, so long as the word cannot then be confused with another. However, if you were singing in a period accent, such as in a Noel Coward musical, you might need to make clear all three sounds in the word.

5. Consider the requirements of style when choosing how to time the transition from one sound to the next in compound vowels. Here are some examples of stylistic differences:

i. In preparing a song from a classic book musical such as '*I Could have Danced all Night*' from *My Fair Lady* by Lerner and Lowe, the first sound will be held longer than the second and the transition between first and second sound will be slow and gradual.

[na   ɪ   t]

ii. In a more contemporary musical such as *Jekyll and Hyde* by Wildhorn and Bricusse, the transition will be managed differently: the essential difference is that the change is faster, more abrupt, happening either halfway or two-thirds of the way through the written note value. This can give a feel of heightened drama.

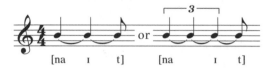

[na   ɪ   t]   [na   ɪ   t]

iii. In preparing a rock and roll number for *Smokey Joe's Café* the treatment would be different again: vowels in popular music are closest to those of Southern American because of the roots of the musical style. In this example there is no transition at all because only the first vowel is sung; the final 't' /t/ is also unaspirated.

[n–a–a–aɪt˺]

In performance, decisions about the above will be made in collaboration with your MD and Director. Once the choices have been made, dealing with compound vowels becomes a matter of timing. You will need to work out how many sounds you have to make within the given note value and plan where to make the transition.

CLARITY OF CONSONANTS

Look at the diagram opposite, showing the places where the vocal tract can be obstructed. The diagram is followed by a breakdown of the 'General English Consonants', including their manner and placement. Sample words are included alongside each category as well as the phonetic symbol. The consonants fall into four categories: plosives (stops), fricatives, approximants (glides), and nasals.

The categories tell you *how* the consonants are made; placement (as shown in the diagram opposite and described on the chart) tells you *where*. In addition to this, consonants may be either voiced or unvoiced.

Placement

The places where the vocal tract can be obstructed are numbered.

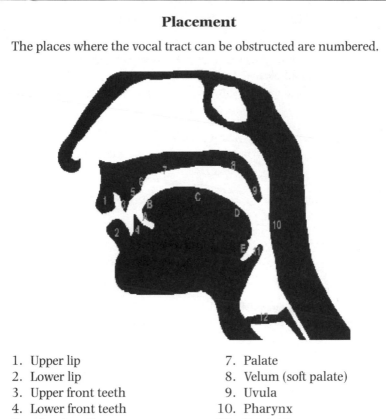

1. Upper lip
2. Lower lip
3. Upper front teeth
4. Lower front teeth
5. Alveolar ridge
6. Postalveolar region
7. Palate
8. Velum (soft palate)
9. Uvula
10. Pharynx
11. Epiglottis
12. Glottis

The places of articulation used in standard speech are 1, 2, 3, 5, 6, 7, 8 and 12.

The letters indicate parts of the tongue: the tip (A), blade (B). front (C), back (D) and root (E).

Using this information you will be able to work out which muscles are required for clarity of consonants. Read the sample words from the chart out loud so that you can begin to develop a visual, auditory and muscular memory for the sounds.

Consonants are sometimes neglected in singing training, largely because they are more difficult to manage in singing than vowels. For example, you cannot sing on a stopped consonant such as 't', only before

General English Consonants

Bilabial
/p/   voiceless bilabial plosive: as in **p**eel, a**pp**roach, stoo**p**
/b/   voiced bilabial plosive: as in **b**ell, tri**b**ute, tu**b**e
/m/   voiced bilabial nasal: as in **m**arry, ca**m**paign, handso**m**e

Labiodental
/f/   voiceless labiodental fricative as in **f**ellow, a**f**ter, stu**ff**
/v/   voiced labiodental fricative: as in **v**ery, a**v**erage, gi**v**e

Labial-velar
/w/   voiced labial-velar approximant: as in **w**estern, stal**w**art, a**w**ay

Dental
/θ/   voiceless dental fricative: as in **th**ink, a**th**lete, tru**th**
/ð/   voiced dental fricative: as in **th**is, ra**th**er, soo**th**e

Alveolar
/t/   voiceless alveolar plosive: as in **t**ime, fu**t**ile, ha**t**
/d/   voiced alveolar plosive: as in **d**eep, a**dd**ition, be**d**
/s/   voiceless alveolar fricative: as in **s**ip, a**ss**ume, bli**ss**
/z/   voiced alveolar fricative: as in **z**est, pre**s**ume, head**s**
/l/   voiced alveolar lateral approximant: as in **l**ast, flour, simi**l**ar
/n/   voiced alveolar nasal: as in **n**either, a**n**tique, fu**n**

Postalveolar
/ʃ/   voiceless postalveolar fricative: as in **sh**ift, vi**c**ious, po**sh**
/ʒ/   voiced postalveolar fricative: as in mea**s**ure, fu**s**ion, vi**s**ion
/tʃ/   voiceless postalveolar affricate: as in **ch**est, a**ch**ieve, lur**ch**
/dʒ/   voiced postalveolar affricate: as in **j**ump, a**dj**acent, ba**dge**
/r/   voiced postalveolar approximant: as in **r**ed, a**rr**ow, **r**u**r**al

Palatal
/j/   voiced palatal approximant: as in **y**esterday, can**y**on, vine**y**ard

Velar
/k/   voiceless velar plosive: as in **k**ept, sil**k**en, sha**ck**
/g/   voiced velar plosive: as in **g**uest, be**g**otten, bi**g**
/ŋ/   voiced velar nasal: as in si**ng**, li**n**k, Li**n**coln

Glottal
/h/   voiceless glottal fricative: as in **h**ave, a**h**ead, **h**uge

or after it. This means that you need to allow your voice to stop when executing the 't', which in turn changes the airflow. Audibility of consonants is also a key issue, affecting the communication link between you and the listener.

Consonants routines

Singers need exercises for working consonants as well as vowels. Here are two that I commonly use with my clients. They are followed by an awareness exercise using sung text.

Exercise 1: PITCHING AND MUSCULARITY

This first exercise enables you to develop control and flexibility in the muscles of articulation and gets you used to pitching voiced consonants.
1. Sing five vowels to each consonant and work through all the consonants listed on the chart on page 142. (Omit 'w', 'r' and 'y' for the moment.)
2. Start as slowly as you need and work up the scale.

/diː/ /de/ daː/ /dɔː/ /duː/   /diː/ /de/ daː/ /dɔː/ /duː/   /diː/

3. Focus your attention on specific placement of the consonants.
4. With the voiced consonants (e.g. 'm' 'v' and 'z'), pitch on each note of the scale as you go up.
5. With the voiceless consonants (e.g. 'p' 't' and 'f'), form the sounds before each beat in the sequence. Do not try to open out much when you sing the vowels; there isn't time.
6. Increase the number of beats and, gradually, the speed, by doing three beats on each note of the scale:

/di: di: di: de de de daː: daː: daː: dɔː dɔː dɔː duː/   /di: di: di: de de de ...

You will find this easier to do if you increase your effort for the build-up to the first note in each of the triplets. The other two sounds will bounce off that first effort.

Monitor how and where the consonants are made:
i. Making an 'f' requires work in the lips and friction in the breath stream;
ii. Making a 'k' requires work in the soft palate (velum) and tongue. The breath is first held, then released;

iii. Making a 'z' requires work in the tongue against the alveolar ridge. There is some friction in the breath;

iv. Making an 'l' requires work in the tongue on the alveolar ridge, and the breath is continuous.

7. Take a breath whenever you need it in this exercise. It will be easy to recoil.

8. Monitor the larynx for constriction, and use the silent laugh.

Exercise 2: RELEASING VOICED CONSONANTS

With voiced consonants, activity is going on in three places: the point of obstruction, the vocal folds, and the breath. You need to coordinate all three to make a clean ending to a word or syllable that finishes on one of these sounds.

1. Practise singing voiced fricatives in pairs 'v'–'v', 'th'–'th', 'z'–'z', and so on.

2. Notice what is needed to stop the sound between each pair: the breath stream needs to stop, the vocal folds need to open, and the consonant obstruction (tongue and hard palate, lips and teeth, tongue and teeth) needs to be released.

3. Practise singing on one note up the scale words or phrases that involve voiced fricatives, nasals and the lateral approximant 'l' /l/. For example, 'maybe this time' (ending with a nasal consonant) or 'the autumn leaves' (ending with a voice fricative).

i. Maintain the shape of the consonant (point of obstruction) until you have finished the note. If you release it before you have finished singing, you will make a vowel at the end of the word.

ii. Come off voice by opening your vocal folds.

iii. Stop the breath stream from the abdomen by recoiling with the breath.

Awareness exercise: AN UP-TEMPO PATTER SONG

Patter songs are an excellent exercise in consonant articulation. During this exercise, focus on where and how the consonants are made, referring to the placement diagram and chart (pages 141–2) if you need to. Here are the first four lines of text of Sondheim's 'Everybody says Don't' from the musical *Anyone Can Whistle*. You can work the song with the melody as well.

> **Everybody says Don't,**
> **Everybody says Don't,**
> **Everybody say Don't, it isn't right,**
> **Don't, it isn't nice.**

1. Speak the lines at your normal speaking pace.
2. Now extract only the consonants: 'v'–'r'–'b' and so on. Give yourself time to process this stage by working at thinking and feeling speed. Do not try to make the vowels; they will come anyway when you release the consonants, but don't spend any time on them. (Note that the letter 'y' stands for a vowel in this passage.)
3. Speak the passage again, working the consonants a little harder and making them well defined. Avoid gripping the jaw or over-working it during this stage. Simply focus on which muscles are involved in making the consonants.
i.   Allow twice as much time for all the fricatives, e.g. 'v', 'z', 's'.
ii. Spend longer in the build-up to the stop for stopped consonants, e.g. 't'.
iii. Double the volume of your nasal consonants wherever they appear in the word, e.g. 'n'.
4. Now introduce the melody. Sing the passage at half speed, or slower if you need it. Don't worry about the volume you normally get from the vowels; just concentrate on the consonants.

Consonants and context

What happens when you start to work the consonants into the music? Are there any specific musical or vocal issues that arise? In my experience there are a number. You may not need to address all of these issues, but it is as well to be aware of them. Use the following list for troubleshooting.

1. Jaw work in consonants
Consonants are not made with the jaw, though the positioning of some points of articulation require the jaw to be moved. You will find it helpful to monitor your jaw movement during consonant work, so that the muscles of articulation can work efficiently.
i. Look in a mirror or place a finger on your chin as described in Chapter 6, page 61. Notice that the jaw needs to close to make some sounds. If your singing training has been vowel based, you will need to get used to this.
ii. Check where the consonants are made using the placement diagram (page 141). Using the consonant routines described in Exercises 1–2 monitor extraneous jaw movements while aiming for clarity of consonants.

2. Breath use in consonants
i. Pay attention to changes in your airflow and pressure, as well as to how and when you breathe in. Fricatives require more breath use in their execution; plosives require the breath to be stopped.
ii. You can breathe in on the aspiration that follows voiceless stops such as 't' /t/, 'p' /p/, 'k' /k/, 's' /s/ and 'CH' /ʧ/.

3. Constriction in consonants

Constriction can occur when you are unclear about where the consonants are made. This is particularly true for the voiced consonants where there may be confusion between effort levels in voicing and effort levels in the breath needed for the type of sound. An example would be in singing a word like 'George', which has a voiced affricate 'j' /ʤ/ (a combination of a voiced stop and a voiced fricative) at the beginning and the end. Here the breath is obstructed in several places in the vocal tract: at the vocal folds (voicing), and at the alveolar and the post-alveolar regions. This can cause breath to 'back up' in the vocal tract, which in turn might lead to constriction in the larynx. Because singing requires us to sustain pitch, you are more likely to constrict on the voiced stops, fricatives and affricates in singing than in speech.

i. Use the diagram and table on pages 141 and 142 to clarify where the work is needed for these consonants.

ii. Monitor your breath use, making sure that you use enough breath to make the consonant clearly but that you do not push air into the sound.

iii. Practise forming the consonants with the silent laugh in place. Speak the sound and then sing the sound, holding the effort level of retraction.

4. Pitching of voiced consonants

You need to voice the consonant on the pitch of the note you are about to sing. This includes voiced fricatives, approximants, nasals and voiced stops. If you don't do this strange scooping noises may ensue!

i. Prepare the pitch by sirening it. Then make the consonant on the same pitch.

ii. An exception to this guideline would be in singing pop, where pitch glides are part of the vocal style.

5. Finishing voiced consonants

With voiced consonants there is sometimes a danger of adding an extra vowel between words. Consider this line from the ballad '*Time Heals Everything*' by Jerry Herman: 'And one fine morning the hurt will end.' If voicing is continued at the ends of words, the following might result: 'and-uh one fine-uh morning-uh the hurt will mend'. This is more likely to happen with singers who are trained in traditional 'bel canto' technique, and when singing ballads rather than up-tempi songs.

i. To avoid this, open your vocal folds after the end of the nasal consonants. You needn't breath in; just open the folds.

ii. The same strategy can be used for any final voiced consonants.

6. Audibility in nasal consonants

Nasal consonants sound loud inside our head but are quieter outside; this is because they are filtered through the nasal cavity. You need to balance the volume of your nasal consonants to match that of the vowels. Explore the following with a partner:

i. Put your hands over your ears and sing 'many many men' on one note. Notice that the vowels sound quieter than the consonants.

ii. Ask your partner to sing the same phrase. Notice that, from outside, the vowels are louder than the consonants.

iii. Ask your partner to increase volume on the nasal consonants until the sound is balanced for you, the listener.

iv. Ask your partner to quantify the increase in effort required to make the consonants match the vowels in volume.

v. Repeat stages ii-iv, with your partner giving you feedback.

7. Making time for the consonants

The timing of consonants in sung text is probably one of the most important issues that a singer needs to address. Many singers are used to giving the whole note value to the vowel in a word or syllable. When you start to make more of the consonants, you have to make room for them within the note value so that you do not upset the rhythm.

i. Initial consonants need to be made before the beat.

ii. Final consonants need to be made within the beat.

Here is a short extract from Sondheim's '*Anyone Can Whistle*' with the timing for the consonants written in:

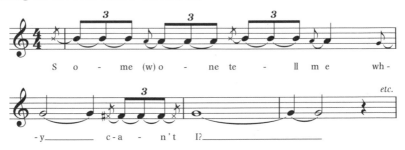

If you are used to singing 'on the vowels' this will feel odd at first. Essentially what you are doing is allotting some of the note value to the consonants instead of just to the vowel. In Chapter 13, pages 182–3 there is a music score showing how this works within the rhythmic structure of a song.

8. Approximants or glides r /r/, w /w/, y /j/

Listed above are three of the four approximants of General British and American. These sounds are so called because there is no true point of obstruction. For the purposes of singing, treat these sounds as you would compound vowels by singing all the transitions that are present in the sounds on the pitch of the note. In doing this you will find it helpful to think of the 'vowel' that goes with each sound, e.g. 'OO' /uː/ for 'w' /w/, 'EE' /iː/ for 'y' /j/, and 'uh' /ə/ for 'r' /r/. Look at example (a).

(a)

i. Sing the word 'world' slowly. Treat the first sound in the word as 'OO' /uː/.

ii. You need to pitch the 'OO' on the note you are singing. Then:

iii. Move from the 'OO' /uː/ into the vowel 'ER' /ɜː/ or 'URR' /ɝː/ (U.S.).

iv. Note the change of position in the lips from rounded to neutral as you move into the main target vowel 'ER' /ɜː/ or 'URR' /ɝː/(U.S.).

The musical example shows a suggested timescale for this.

Now look at example (b).

(b)

Ro – mance___

i. Sing 'romance' and notice what is happening with your tongue as you form the 'r'. In General British the first sound in 'r' at the beginning of a word will be like the schwa 'uh' /ə/. You need to pitch the 'r' just before the written beat, and then sing the main vowel on the beat. (The little note with a line through it indicates when you need to sing the consonant.)

ii. Treating the 'r' as a vowel means you can medialise, so prepare this sound with your tongue in the ready position.

9. Syllabic consonants

In General British, example words containing syllabic consonants include 'button' and 'people'. Phonetically these two words would be transcribed thus: [bʌtn] and [piːpɫ]. In speech, the second syllable in each case is minimised because it is unstressed. In certain music settings, this relationship can become unbalanced.

Consider this music extract from '*People*' from *Funny Girl* by Jule Styne.

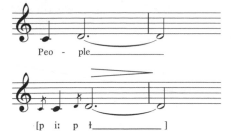

i. Aim to make a decrease in tone during the second syllable of the word (the long note).

ii. Pitch the final 'll' /ł/ on the written note, and sing the entire note value on the consonant without inserting a vowel.

The decrease in tone, which in speech happens naturally between the stressed and unstressed syllable, needs to be matched in the sung note. This phenomenon of decreasing tone to balance the stress of syllables is known as 'decay'.

TEXT AND MEANING

As a matter of course, an experienced actor will usually balance the musical setting of the text with the semantic and interpretive meaning. Those less experienced may fall into the trap of singing well but not really meaning the text. This is not simply to do with emotional connection; it also has to do with understanding how to make the words work for you within the structure of the music. Inflection and meaning of text can be upset or distorted in a number of ways:

1. by changing the vowels;

2. by running words together;

3. by unbalancing the stress of a syllable, word or phrase.

Some of these problems can arise from the setting of the music. Even so, you can choose to interpret the musical text so that the written text remains intelligible. Examples of problems **2** and **3** are given below, with solutions. Problem **1** has already been dealt with earlier in this chapter.

1. Running words together

It is very tempting when singing a ballad to run words into each other. This can happen if you get caught up in the melody or in the generalised emotional content of the song. Remember that, in musical theatre, text has priority over voice, even in great ballads such as Jerry Herman's '*Time*

Heals Everything' from *Mac and Mabel*. Here, a simple but memorable melody is repeated in a rising sequence. How can you get the audience to really listen to what you are saying when you sing this, rather than being seduced by the melody? Look at the first four lines:

Time heals everything, Tuesday, Thursday,
Time heals everything, April, August,
If I'm patient, the break will mend,
And one fine morning the hurt will end.

i.   Read the text aloud in an ordinary speech rhythm. Mean what you say as you say it. If you do this, you will instinctively put the commas in, which means breaking the vocal line.
ii.   Make sure you stress the all-important word 'ev'rything' by putting a glottal stop at the beginning of it. As well as separating this word from the previous one, it puts a musical and vocal underlining to the word 'everything'. The glottal gives you an opportunity to signal Mabel's emotional state to the audience.
iii. Sing the passage, putting in all the commas and using the glottal onset for words beginning with a vowel that you want to stress ('everything', 'April', 'August', 'if', and so on). When you make the commas, don't worry about breathing in; the recoil will happen naturally when you make the stop. The momentary silence is also an opportunity for the audience to process the emotional content of words and melody.

You don't have to use a glottal onset for every word that begins with a vowel; you can use a simultaneous onset if you prefer a softer attack. In speech it is conventional to insert a glottal before a vowel if the word or syllable is stressed. However, remember that stress is relative: if everything is stressed, then, in effect, nothing is stressed. So whether or not you choose to separate words with a glottal onset is actually an interpretive decision. What is important in singing is that you do not run words into each other, making nonsense of the text ('ti-meal-sev'rything').

2. Melodic distortion
Sometimes the composer sets a long note on an unstressed syllable, distorting the natural inflection of the word. Some actors dislike singing ballads for this reason, feeling that they cannot do justice to the text. This tends to happen more often in songs from shows also intended for release as singles. Listen to or sing the text of '*Someone Like You*' from Frank Wildhorn's *Jekyll and Hyde*.

I peer through wind<u>ows</u>,
Watch life go by,
Dream of tomor<u>row</u>
And wonder why

i. The syllables underlined are on long notes and on a rising phrase, so it would be easy to make them stick out in the phrase.

ii. Make a decrescendo on the second syllable of 'wind-<u>ows</u>', between 'dream' and 'of' and on the third syllable of tomorr-<u>ow</u>'.

This balancing of volume levels will enable you to stress the correct syllables and ensure that the audience can be involved in the meaning of the text as well as the generalised emotion.

A further example is '*Over the Rainbow*' by E. Y. Harburg and Harold Arlen, which starts with an octave leap: it is a musical picture of longing expressed through the song. High notes are heard as louder by the human ear; so '-where' will automatically be louder if you do not make an adjustment when singing. By decaying (making a decrescendo) into the second note as shown in the example, you can ensure a natural speech reading of the text. Here's how to manage the decay:

i. All dynamic levels are relative. If you want to belt out the song joyously, that is fine. Alternatively, you may prefer something more wistful and lyrical. Set your levels accordingly.

ii. Make a conscious effort to decrease volume as you approach the top note. This drop in volume needs to happen before you sing the vowel on the top note.

iii. Use the 'm' of 'some-' to help you with the decay; you will automatically get a drop in volume on the nasal 'm' because the sound is being filtered through the nose.

iv. Aim to match the volume of the 'm' with the '-where', and then decay through the rest of the syllable.

An alternative reading of the song, such as the one now made famous by Eva Cassidy and released on the CD *Songbird*, is perfectly viable in a different setting. This reading is essentially a jazz rendition of the song, emphasizing nuances of meaning that are intensely personal to the singer. However, this reading would hold up rather than advance the action in the context of the musical.

There are situations where you may distort the text for stylistic reasons. Examples might include tribute shows such as *Mamma Mia*, in which you would want to inflect the text in the same way as the original recordings, or Jazz or Blues shows, in which the songs may not be intended as dramatic vehicles. This is fine, so long as it is the result of informed choice.

Musical theatre singing is about text first, voice second. If you work with this principle you will find it easier to make songs work for you. Within this principle are five simple guidelines that might summarise the work of this chapter:

1. Sing-as-you-speak in the world and environment of the character.

2. Maintain the integrity of the vowels.

3. Ensure clarity of consonants.

4. Mean what you sing.

5. Make conscious choices about style and delivery.

Chapter 12

Creating voice qualities

When we listen to somebody speaking or singing, we inevitably make judgements about what we hear. These judgements may be based on social, cultural and aesthetic considerations as well as our own psychological responses. Sometimes we will make comparisons with our own voices, wishing that we could 'have a voice like such-and-such'. I have a motto that I reserve for these situations: 'my voice *does*, rather than my voice *is*'. The work in the previous chapters has prepared you for the exciting journey of controlling your own voice quality. Every time you make a sound you are creating a voice quality. By learning the muscular 'set-up' in the vocal tract for certain clearly defined qualities you can develop greater control over your own sound. This is useful in character work, for creating vocal colours, and for changing vocal style. Above all it is empowering.

Look at Diagram 1 of the vocal tract opposite. Nearly everything in the vocal tract is capable of movement: up, down, in and out, forwards, backwards.[1] Only the roof of the mouth has a fixed position. It is this feature that gives you a uniquely flexible instrument, enabling you to manipulate the moveable parts of the vocal tract specifically to produce a range of distinctive sounds.

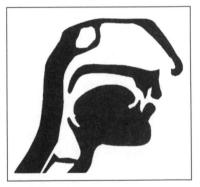

Diagram 1: The vocal tract

The scientific study of specific voice qualities is relatively new. This may be because voice science tends to run behind performance practice. We have had medical techniques for viewing the voice in action for over a century, but it is only relatively recently that information from this type of research has been available to teachers of voice and singing. There are now numerous organisations and societies that foster a multi-disciplinary approach to voice and help disseminate the information to teachers and performers. The initial work that we are going to do in this chapter is based on a theoretical model of voice quality from the American voice

[1] I don't mean to imply that all of the structures move in all these directions. Each structure has a specific range of movement, a topic beyond the remit of this book.

researcher, Jo Estill. Estill was a singer and teacher who in mid-life became interested in voice science. In the course of various research projects she identified six differentiated voice qualities: speech, falsetto, cry/sob, twang, opera and belt. All of these in pure and mixed form are used in musical theatre singing. In this chapter we shall be learning how to create five of these voice qualities. First, let's identify how and when they might be used.

How voice qualities are used

Speech quality. Historically, this quality was used in the verse part of set songs but has become far more widely used. Speech quality, as its name implies, has a natural, direct sound and is a main feature of much popular music as well as musical theatre repertoire. Speech quality is used in narrative and patter songs, point numbers, jazz and pop musicals, and in through-composed works such as *Miss Saigon* and *Jekyll and Hyde*. For examples of speech quality listen to the following recordings:

i. '*Looking at the World Through Rose Coloured Glasses*' performed by Frank Sinatra with the Count Basie Orchestra, Valiant VS 144. This demonstrates speech quality almost throughout the song. Listen especially to the final note.

ii. '*The American Dream*' from *Miss Saigon*, by Alan Boublil and Claude-Michel Schönberg performed by Jonathan Pryce on the Original London Cast recording, First Night Records, WX 329 7599-24271-1, 1988.

iii. '*Imagine My Surprise*' from *Personals*, by Crane, Feidman and Kauffman (book and lyrics) and Dreskin, Friedman (J P and S), Menken, Schwarz and Skloft (music). Performed by Summer Rognlie on the Original London Cast recording, Jay Productions CD, ISBN 05288 13192. Listen to the opening sequence up to the first 'You'.

iv. '*At the End of the Day*' from *Les Misérables*, by Alain Boublil and Claude-Michel Schönberg, performed by the company on the Original London Cast recording, First Night Records, ISBN 014636 100121. A good example of speech quality in ensemble singing.

Falsetto quality. Falsetto quality can be made by both men and women and is useful for moments of vulnerability, intimacy and uncertainty. This is not a projecting voice quality, but it works well in musical theatre where amplification is now the norm. For examples of falsetto quality listen to the following recordings:

i. The opening lines and last two bars of '*Bring Him Home*' from '*Les Misérables*' by Alain Boublil and Claude-Michel Schönberg, performed by Colm Wilkinson on the Original Cast recording, First Night Records, ISBN 014636100121.

ii. The final sixteen bars of '*Squeeze me*' by Fats Waller on the Original Broadway Cast recording of *Ain't Misbehavin'* RCA BL82965(2).

iii. '*Stay With Me*' from *Into the Woods* by Stephen Sondheim, performed by Bernadette Peters on the Original Cast recording, RCA Victor, ISBN 7863-56796-1. Listen to the section beginning 'don't you know what's out there in the woods?'

Cry quality. When you are singing ballads, your sound needs to be warm and approachable. This is cry quality. Cry is the basis of 'legit' singing, and it is a must for ballads in classic book musicals, though not limited to these. Cry is also used in situations that call for depth of feeling and expression of romantic passion in any musical genre. For examples of cry quality listen to the following recordings:

i. '*A Dream is a Wish Your Heart Makes*' from Disney's *Cinderella*, music and lyrics by David Mack, Al Hoffman and Jerry Livingston, performed by Barbara Cook on *Barbara Cook the Disney Album*, MCA Records, 76732-6244-2.

ii. '*I'll Tell the Man in the Street*' by Rodgers and Hart sung by Kristin Chenoweth on the CD *Let Yourself Go*, Sony 2001-01-01.

iii. '*Send in the Clowns*' from *A Little Night Music* by Stephen Sondheim performed by Mandy Patinkin on *Mandy Patinkin Sings Sondheim*, Nonesuch 79690 – 2. Listen to the bridge 'just when I'd stopped opening doors'.

Twang quality. Twang adds brilliance and edge to any vocal set-up and is therefore invaluable in performance situations. Twang is often indicated in roles that are comic, frenetic or neurotic. For examples of twang quality listen to the following recordings:

i. '*Take Back your Mink*' from *Guys and Dolls* by Frank Loesser, performed by Kim Criswell on *Guys and Dolls, Selected Highlights*, Show, CD034.

ii. '*Sit Down, You're Rocking the Boat*' from *Guys and Dolls* by Frank Loesser, performed by Don Stephenson on *Guys and Dolls, Selected Highlights*, Show, CD034.

iii. '*The Girl in 14g*' by Jeanine Tesori and Dick Scanlan, performed by Kristin Chenoworth on the CD *Let Yourself Go* Sony 2001-01-01. The opening sequence to 'a perfect nook...' demonstrates that twang can be cute as well as brash in the female voice.

Opera quality. Certain roles or songs in musical theatre require an operatic voice quality. *Carmen Jones* is an obvious example, as are those musicals that fall into the operetta or musical comedy categories such as *Showboat* or *Bitter Sweet*. For examples of an operatic voice quality in musical theatre, listen to:

i. The verse of '*Music of the Night*' from *Phantom of the Opera* by Andrew Lloyd Webber, Charles Hart and Richard Stilgo, sung by Anthony Warlow on *Centre Stage*, Polydore 847 4342.

ii. '*My Joe*' from *Carmen Jones* by Oscar Hammerstein II and Georges Bizet, performed by Karen Parks on the Original London Cast recording, EMI CDC7543512

iii. '*Springtime for Hitler*' from *The Producers* by Mel Brooks and Thomas Meehan, performed by Eric Gunhus on the Original Broadway Cast recording, Sony Classical ISBN 099708 964627. Listen to the first solo sequence which is sung in Operetta style.

(6) **Belt quality.** Traditionally belting was used by certain character roles in musicals, usually the funny, quirky or feisty female roles. Now belting is more prevalent and is used by both men and women. Belting is the vocal equivalent of situations and emotions 'in extremis' and can be used to express a range of heightened feelings: joy, despair, anger, frustration, exuberance, and so on. Rock and gospel musicals also require belting as part of the vocal and musical style. For examples of Belting, listen to:

i. '*Our Kind of Love*' from *The Beautiful Game* by Andrew Lloyd Webber and Ben Elton, performed by Josie Walker on the Original London Cast recording Telstar TCD3160. Listen to the section starting 'I will strive for peace with all my might', culminating in 'that's what's right'.

ii. '*I'm Always True to You Darlin' in my Fashion*' from *Kiss me Kate* by Cole Porter, performed by Amy Spanger, DRG Records CD 12988, 2000.

iii. '*Over the Rainbow*' by Harold Arlen and E.Y. Harburg, performed by Sam Harris on Mowtown Records 6103 MCLP, 1984. Listen to the final rendition of 'somewhere' and to the coda 'why can't I?'

iv. '*Oh, Had I a Golden Thread*' by Pete Seeger, performed by Eva Cassidy on *Songbird*, Didgeridoo G2-10045. Listen to the section beginning 'won't you show my brothers and sisters' leading to ' 'cos I will bind up the sorry world' and 'always' for high belting.

v. '*Heaven On Their Minds*' from *Jesus Christ Superstar* by Andrew Lloyd Webber and Tim Rice, performed by Clive Rowe, TER CD MUS C N29, 1995. Listen to the section starting 'Jesus!' continuing to 'your talk of God is true'.

vi. '*When You Got It, Flaunt It*' from *The Producers* by Mel Brooks, performed by Cady Huffman on the Original Broadway Cast recording Sony ISBN 5099708964627. Listen to the section after 'now Ulla belt'.

THE PARAMETERS FOR CHANGING VOICE QUALITY

Each quality is the result of a configuration of muscles and structures in the vocal tract. This is what I mean by the term 'vocal set-up'. Here are the structures we shall be moving in order to change set-up. You have already learned how to control each of them in earlier chapters of the book.

Your vocal set-up

In the larynx:
Vocal Fold Activity: thick or thin; raised plane position (see Chapters 3 and 7)
Laryngeal Posture: height, tilt (see Chapter 3)

In the resonators:
Nasal port: open, closed or half-open (see Chapter 6)
Aryepiglottic region: relaxed or tightened (see Chapter 9)
Tongue positioning: body medialised or low, or back high or low (see Chapter 8)

In the support mechanism:
Body: vocal tract relaxed or anchored; torso relaxed or anchored (see Chapter 7)
Breath use: airflow high or low, and subglottic pressure higher or lower (see Chapter 4)

The specific features of each voice quality are set out below with an indication of where they work most easily in the vocal range. Refer to work on range in Chapter 5 if you need to remind yourself about managing gear changes in the range (pages 50 and 51).

Speech quality is characterised by thick vocal folds and a neutral larynx position. Subglottic pressure is high in speech quality, so breath management is important. The sound is 'thick', 'intense', 'heavy', and projects well. Speech quality works most easily below the first gear change in both male and female voices, but it can safely be taken higher with practice.

Falsetto quality is characterised by a raised vocal fold plane, with the vocal folds vibrating but not closing, which means it does not project well. As in speech quality the larynx position is neutral. Subglottic pressure is minimal in falsetto quality, so it is not breath efficient. The sound quality is more diffuse than speech quality and may also be breathy. Falsetto quality works most easily above the gear change in the mid-high range.

③ **Cry quality** is characterised by a tilted larynx (the thyroid cartilage is tilted forward) and thin vocal folds. The larynx is in rest or high position, depending on the pitch. Subglottic pressure is lower than in speech quality but higher than in falsetto. Breath use will feel balanced and 'controlled'. The sound is quiet, clear and somewhat rounded in quality. It will usually have vibrato. This quality is usually accessed above the first gear change, but it can be brought down into the lower range with effect.

A variation of cry quality is sob, where the larynx is lowered. Because of the lower laryngeal position you will need to stabilise the head and neck in sob. Sob is dark, quiet and intense.

④ **Twang quality** is characterised by a tightened aryepiglottic sphincter with high larynx and tongue. The thyroid can be tilted or neutral, allowing for a thinner or thicker vocal fold mass. The tightening of the aryepiglottis tends to increase resistance in the vocal folds, so it is important not to drive breath in this voice quality. Twang can also be nasal or oral. Twang is edgy, brilliant and piercing, and it can be added to other qualities to introduce the 'singer's formant' for ease of projection across the range.

These are all simple voice qualities. The next two voice qualities are complex in their set-up.

⑤ **Belting** is a mix of speech and twang with a high larynx and tilted cricoid. The tilted cricoid (the lower section of the laryngeal cartilage) helps you to sing high notes with thick folds without traumatising the voice. Because the vocal folds are staying together longer, subglottic pressure is high. It is important not to push air in this voice quality. Belting is made above Middle E or F (330–349 Hertz) in both the male and female voice.

⑥ **Opera quality** is a mix of speech and twang but with a tilted thyroid and lowered larynx. The tilted thyroid reduces the vocal fold mass somewhat, and the lowered larynx balances the brightness of twang with some depth and 'covering'. Closest to opera quality in musical theatre singing is cry quality, the basis of 'legit' singing. The operatic set-up is probably the most difficult to manage since it involves work in several opposing muscle groups. Subglottic pressure will vary according to volume levels, and singers using opera quality need to negotiate the gear changes with care so that the quality is matched across the range.

What I have described are six possible voice qualities. Think of them as a reference point for creating and identifying primary colours. All of these voice qualities can be mixed with others, and this is how they are used most often in performance. Learning to create the qualities unmixed will enable you to increase your understanding of your own voice and to build reliable muscle feedback. In the exercises that follow we will be working to create the voice qualities that are most used in musical theatre: speech, falsetto, cry, twang and belting. At the end of this chapter, there are suggestions for exploring voice qualities as interpretive tools in preparation for the work in Chapter 13.

Awareness exercise: EXPLORING YOUR VOCAL SET-UP

In the course of many public workshops and private coaching sessions, I have found it invaluable to identify changes in the set-up of spoken voice before working on the singing voice. Here is an exercise to raise awareness of your own habitual vocal patterns. Work the exercise with at least two other people.

1. Read aloud from a newspaper or book; the text needs to be non-dramatic prose.
2. Immediately after you have read aloud, sing or intone the first line of the text.
3. Aim to pitch your singing close to where you pitched your speaking voice.
4. Aim to keep the same feel and sound quality as in speaking; the only difference is that you are now holding pitch.

Monitoring:
i. How would you describe the feel and sound of your speaking voice?
ii. What did you notice changing when you started to sing?
iii. Did you put on a special voice?
iv. Ask the listeners how close your singing voice was to your speaking voice.
v. Using the chart on page 157, work out where in your vocal tract you might have made changes.
vi. What changes were there in general body posture and facial expression?

5. Turn the concept of the exercise around by singing a few lines from a song that you like. Then speak, using the same voice that you used to sing.
6. Take some time to discuss what you have done when everyone in the group has had their turn.

Exercise 1: STEPS TO SPEECH QUALITY

A glottal onset is helpful in setting up speech quality. Auditory cues are 'uh-oh' and speaking in a bored monotone. Use *Amazing Grace* as your practice song.

1. In spoken voice, practise doing a few glottal onsets, first on 'uh-oh' and then on other vowels, sustaining the second sound each time. Play with pitch as you do this, starting on notes higher and lower in your speaking range.
2. Speak the words of the song in a bored monotone, elongating the words a little more than for normal speech.
3. Now speak the first two words (or syllables) of each phrase and sing the rest.

A - maz - ing____   grace,   how   sweet   the   sound

You will find this easier if you pitch close to your speaking voice.

Monitoring:

i. Make sure you are not tilting the thyroid. Do a pitch-slide down on a siren and deliberately 'let go' as you approach the bottom of your range. Before you arrive at your bottom note, allow your voice to relax into a gentle creak, imitating the sound of a creaky door. The feel needs to be very laid back and lazy. This will usually release any thyroid tilt.
ii. Allow the breath to build up before the glottal onset. Practise a few voiced fricatives, and then repeat the onsets with sustained notes. Use the 'diamond of support' to keep the breath pressure sufficient while sustaining speech quality.
iii. If you are not used to the feel of speech quality it may feel forced. Silently laugh to retract the false vocal folds.

A variation of speech quality is breathy speech, in which some air is allowed into the sound but the vocal fold plane is not raised. You are more likely to go into this mode from Falsetto when approaching the bottom of your range.

Exercise 2: STEPS TO FALSETTO QUALITY

Below are the opening lines of a well known song '*The Way You Look Tonight*' by Jerome Kern and Dorothy Fields. Sing the song in the style of Fred Astaire or Bing Crosbie.

Some day when I'm awf'ly low,
When the world is cold,
I will feel a glow just thinking of you,
And the way you look tonight.
Oh, but you're lovely, with your smile so warm,
And your cheek so soft,
There is nothing for me but to love you,
Just the way you look tonight.

An aspirate onset is helpful in setting up falsetto quality. Auditory cues are an English 'Yoo-hoo' or an owl's hoot.

1. Imitate an owl's hoot or call out 'yoo-hoo' in a posh English voice. (If you have ever seen the character Hyacinth Bucket in *Keeping Up Appearances*, you will know exactly what do to.)
2. Aim for a girlish and rather hooty sound quality (the men need to do this too).
3. Keeping the same feel and sound, start to speak the words of the song. You will probably be above your normal speaking range so bring the pitch down a little if you like.
4. Speak one line, then sing one line, aiming to maintain the same vocal set-up. You will find falsetto quality easier around or above your first gear change (women) and above your second gear change (men).

Monitoring:

i. Check that you are in raised plane position for the vocal folds. Slide down in pitch from the highest note in the song, trying to keep the volume the same. If your voice cracks towards the bottom of your range you were in raised plane position. If not, review Exercise 6 from Chapter 3.
ii. Falsetto is not breath efficient. If you are pushing too much air, or if the sound is too breathy or your throat starts to feel dry, reduce your airflow by releasing the breath more slowly.
iii. Falsetto isn't great for long term use. It may work well in the recording studio, but it can be vocally tiring if used in other situations. Make sure your use of falsetto is appropriate to the space you are working in.

There are numerous variants of falsetto, including falsetto with thyroid tilt and falsetto with twang. Many popular music singers currently move between falsetto, speech and breathy speech, using the plane flip as a stylistic device. (Listen to Dido, Alanis Morissette, and Craig David).

Exercise 3: STEPS TO CRY QUALITY

Work with '*Amazing Grace*'.

A simultaneous onset is helpful in setting up cry quality. Auditory cues are a 'little girl voice' and an 'oh dear, sorry voice'.

1. Siren up and down a little to access thin vocal folds. Make sure that the sound is quiet.
2. Make some whimpering or moaning noises on vowels. You will find this easier to do above your first gear change.
3. Speak the words of the song around this pitch, keeping the same sound and feeling as in whimpering and moaning. Notice that this is not your normal speaking voice.
4. Come down gradually in pitch so that you can make this sound quality in the middle of your range.
5. Sing a few notes of the song, keeping the same set-up.

Monitoring:

i. Speaking in this mode can sound fake. Stay with it. This set-up is not usual for speaking voice but is ideal for cry quality.
ii. You may need to stabilise the vocal tract. Line up the axis and atlas joints using the head pat from Chapter 7, page 77.
iii. Airflow against thin vocal folds needs to be balanced and controlled; torso anchoring will help.

6. Sing the whole song on a siren.
7. Miren the song, mouthing the words but keeping the 'ng'/ŋ/ siren at the back of the mouth.
8. Sing the song on the vowels only, making sure that the nasal port is closed.
9. Finally, sing the song with the words.

Cry unmixed is quiet. It can also feel quite effortful if you are not used to singing 'legit'. Cry can be used throughout the upper range to access high notes quietly. It can also be mixed with other qualities to add sweetness.

A variant of cry is 'sob'. Sob is made with thin folds, a tilted thyroid and a lowered larynx. Further anchoring is needed with sob to stabilise the vocal tract. Sob is used to produce depth of tone in some styles of classical singing.

Exercise 4: STEPS TO TWANG QUALITY

Work with '*Amazing Grace*'.

The preparation for twang is similar to that of cry. Use thin folds and a simultaneous onset. The setting for the larynx is high in twang, which is different from cry. Auditory cues are the taunting child ('nyea-nyea-nyea-nyea-nyea'), a cackling witch, a quacking duck or a yowling cat.

1. Begin by sirening up to a high note in your range: note that the larynx and tongue are high and that you have tilted the thyroid. Hold this posture silently as you breathe in and out through the nose.
2. Make a small meow, like the cry of a pathetic kitten. Notice that you need hardly open your jaw to do this. Your effort level in the folds should be minimal, i.e. thin folds. Make a series of small mewing sounds like this.
3. Now increase the volume, imitating the sound of the cat yowling. Notice the sense of increased pressure behind the nose.
4. Turn the meow into a longer 'nyeeow'. Initiating the tone with 'n' instead of 'm' will help you to keep the tongue high.
5. Practise the sound on different notes in your range and on different vowel sounds, noticing any adjustments you need to make or any changes in effort levels.
6. Practise speaking the words of the song in this mode. If this is not your normal speaking mode it may feel thin or small and sound piercing and shrill.
7. Now sing the entire song using 'nyeeow', making sure the sound is bright and twangy.
8. Insert a 'ny' /nj/ before each vowel in the song, and repeat the melody.
9. Sing the words in twang.

Monitoring:
i. Twang is a form of constriction above the vocal folds. Make sure you are retracting the false vocal folds in this mode.
ii. Both your tongue and larynx need to be kept high in this voice quality. Use the monitoring devices from Exercise 3, Chapter 3 (page 21) and Exercises 3 and 4 for medialising the vowels in Chapter 8 to help you. The sensation of twang is 'small space'.
iii. Twang is most easily accessed with the nasal port half open. For oral twang, review Exercise 6, Chapter 9 (page 116).

Twang can be used as a voice quality in its own right. It can also be used to boost sound levels in other voice qualities, including cry, speech and falsetto. Twang works well across the range, though is rarely used at the very top in the female voice (above soprano high A 880 Hertz) since it is usually unnecessary to boost sound levels at this pitch range. Twang may be used in crossing the gear changes in both directions, and it is especially helpful in blending the vocal registers (see below). Twang is a component of many US accents, which may account for its prevalence in musical theatre singing.

Voice quality, registers and range

Singers who are used to working with 'chest and head' register terminology will recognise a relationship between speech quality and chest register, and cry quality and head register. Thereafter things become more complex. What is twang? Is it more like head register or chest register? And how does falsetto fit into the picture?

Broadly speaking, the term 'register' refers to a range of pitch having a consistent timbre or quality. In this sense we could say that the voice qualities are like distinct vocal registers. However, in singing the concept of register is concerned mainly with a change in voice quality *at particular pitches*, due to changes in the vocal mechanism. In Chapters 5 and 7 we spent some time exploring these changes and learning how to manage them in range work. (See Exercises 3 and 4, Chapter 5 (page 48) and Exercises 6 to 9, Chapter 7 (pages 87–8)). In working with the voice qualities you will still need to negotiate the gear changes, but you may well do it differently and perhaps in a different part of your range. This means that you will have many more options for singing in the middle of your range.

'Blending' or 'mixing' is considered necessary in some styles of music because the voice is an imperfect instrument acoustically. It neither feels nor sounds the same across the range. By judiciously blending voice qualities in certain parts of the your range, you can choose to disguise the changes in quality that tend to occur between the vocal registers. Blending to make the voice sound the same throughout the range is not nearly so important in musical theatre singing as in classical singing. Because musical theatre is text-driven, changes in voice quality can be advantageous, allowing you to signal changes of emotional intent to the audience.

Belting as a vocal register

If you have been used to thinking of your range falling into distinct registers (head and chest, or head and falsetto), then you will find it helpful to think of belting as being a further vocal register. Belting should not be confused with 'chest voice' as it happens above the range of notes normally considered to be accessible in chest register. We shall be discussing belting in more detail in the next section.

ADVANCED WORK IN VOICE QUALITY

So far we have learned the voice qualities unmixed. This will enable you to gain familiarity with the sensations and sounds associated with the four basic 'colours' of speech, falsetto, cry and twang. You will have noticed that each vocal set-up is more likely to occur naturally in certain parts of your range. Advancing the voice qualities means taking them across more of the range and negotiating the gear changes. In addition to this we shall be exploring options for complex vocal set-ups that result in mixed voice qualities.

Advancing speech quality

Before advancing speech quality you need to have a good handle on your effort levels in the vocal folds (vocal fold mass). Review work in Chapter 7, Awareness exercise 1 (page 72), to make sure you have a muscle memory for a thick vocal fold mass.

You need to make the following adjustments for taking speech quality across the range:

1. Raise the larynx when you approach your first gear change. This is earlier than normal in both male and female voices. Raising the larynx will enable you to continue on up in speech quality.

2. Stabilise the vocal tract from the sides and from behind (anchoring).

3. Reduce your breath pressure, allowing the sound to become 'smaller'.

4. Monitor the larynx for constriction. (The higher you go, the funnier it needs to be.)

5. Mix your speech with either twang or cry.

Mixing

i. Twang will help you raise the larynx and will make up for any loss of volume as the speech quality gets higher. When mixing twang with speech you need to reduce your effort level in the vocal folds. Review Awareness exercise 2 and Exercise 4, Chapter 7 (pages 73 and 84) for thinning your vocal fold mass. Use speech and twang for contemporary pop and for a bright, hard-edged sound generally. This is not a 'legit' voice quality.

ii. Cry may be mixed with speech by adding some thyroid tilt. This will enable you to use some vibrato on the long notes and add 'roundness' to your tonal quality. You may need to stabilise the vocal tract in this mix.

iii. Speech, cry and twang are commonly used together for dramatic ballad singing in musical theatre. Vocal tract and torso anchoring are required for safe use of this mix.

iv. A further variant of speech quality is breathy speech. This is not the same as falsetto, which is made in the raised plane position. To create breathy speech, begin in straight speech and relax enough to allow slightly more breath flow through the vocal folds. This sound quality is used in jazz, contemporary pop and musical theatre. Be aware that, because the vocal folds are not fully closing, this is not a projecting voice quality.

Using these strategies you will be able to make speech work well for you in songs that go above your first gear change. To the listener it may well sound as though you have not made the gear change. In fact you will have simply managed it differently. For more information about the expected range in speech quality for the different voice types, *Successful Singing Auditions*[2].

Advancing falsetto quality

Maintaining the 'raised plane' position of the vocal folds is the key factor in advancing falsetto quality. If at any time you are not sure about the position of your vocal fold plane, review the work we did in Awareness exercise 8, Chapter 3 (page 25) and Awareness exercise 3, Chapter 7, (page 74).

Make these adjustments for taking falsetto quality across the range:

1. Raise the larynx to access the top of the range as normal.

2. Keep the vocal folds in the raised plane position if you want to use the quality in the lower range, where you would normally change gear 'down'. This can be a vocally unstable position, and it does not project well. Breathy speech is a better option in the lowest third of your vocal range.

3. Adjust your breath flow according to your needs. You do not need to push air into the sound. Too much airflow will tend to make the pitch sharp.

Mixing
i. By mixing cry with falsetto you can reduce some of the breathiness and introduce some vibrato. Start in the raised plane position for the vocal folds, and then tilt the thyroid a little by whimpering or moaning. You will know if you are still in the raised plane position because the airflow is higher than in unmixed cry quality.

This quality is useful for women singing high in jazz numbers and for the old-fashioned Disney sound requiring innocence and sweetness. (Think of the sound quality that might be used in the song '*When You Wish Upon a Star*'.) Men can use this quality to clear breathiness from their falsetto.

ii. To access falsetto with twang, start in the same way, tilting the thyroid a little in raised plane position. Then add some twang. This will add carrying

[2] Successful Singing Auditions, Kayes G, Fisher J, A&C Black Pubs. Ltd. 2002.

power to the falsetto and will make it sound more forceful. This device is used by some classical male falsettists as well as by many pop singers.

Falsetto needs to be a choice. Some singers default to falsetto because they do not let go of the muscles at the back of the larynx responsible for opening the vocal folds. It is important that you are able to close your vocal folds efficiently in vocalising.

Advancing cry quality

To advance cry you need to have a good handle on thyroid tilt and the sensations that go with it. Review the work we did on tilting the thyroid in Awareness exercise 5, Chapter 3 (page 23).
i. Cry can be made louder or softer by adjusting your vocal fold mass and by adding anchoring. This will give the cry quality more 'presence'.
ii. Twang will also add volume to cry quality. In mixing cry and twang, you could experiment with a slightly lower laryngeal position.

There comes a point where a client might ask, 'If I am mixing cry with speech, how do I know if I'm in a speech set-up or a cry set-up?' The short answer to this is that there simply has not been enough research done on voice quality to give a definitive answer. If you have got this far with work on voice quality you will find that your own internal feedback will give you the information you require on the vocal quality you have created. Ultimately, this is what you need to rely on.

FINDING YOUR BELT VOICE

In public workshops I often spend an entire day teaching the set-up for belting. Even then, some people will not be able to do it, though they will leave with a good understanding of what is required to make the sound. Belting requires a dynamic use of the vocal muscles and the supporting structures that can feel alien to some singers. Those who find this voice quality easy will often have habitual speech patterns that are favourable to belting. These patterns would include speaking with thick folds or twang, or both. These speech patterns might be considered 'loud' or 'shrill' in some social environments but regarded as the norm in others.

Those who find it difficult to belt often will speak gently and breathily, and sometimes with a low larynx. Perhaps the biggest inhibitors of belting are the various forms of socialisation that tell us that it is not OK to make a loud noise.

Belting has been described as 'happy yelling' with good reason. The sensation for the singer is similar to that of raising our voice to call out or shout. In this sense belting is very natural, and it can certainly be done by anyone whose voice is healthy. Like the other voice qualities, belting has its own specific set-up.

Key factors in belting

Belt voice quality is based on a mix of speech and twang qualities. However, three key factors make belting distinct from this mix:

1. Look at Diagrams 2–4, showing a change in posture between the thyroid and cricoid cartilages. The ability to access cricoid tilt is a requirement belting voice.

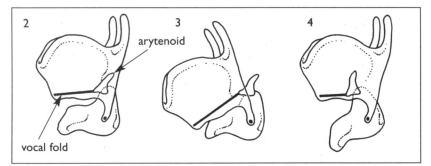

The thyroid and cricoid cartilages: diagram 2 – neutral or rest position, diagram 3 – forward tilt of the thyroid cartilage, and diagram 4 – forward tilt of the cricoid cartilage

2. The photograph shows a postural change outside the larynx in the head-neck relationship. This posture of 'looking up to the gods' is characteristic of many belters.

3. In belting the vocal folds are working very hard, closing forcefully. Research has shown that they spend more time in the closed phase of each vibration than in the open phase. This means that the sound needs *less* breath, even though it is loud. Shallow breathing (as opposed to deep abdominal breathing) is helpful in setting up your belt voice.

Posture for belting: looking up to the Gods

Exercise 5: STEPS TO BELTING

Energised glottal onsets or attacks on 'y' /j/ are helpful in accessing belt quality. On higher pitches, more shallow breathing and a tiny squeak are helpful in the preparation for the sound. Auditory cues are happy yelling ('Eh!' 'Oy!') and your team scoring the winning goal ('Yes'!). Avoid initiating belt notes with an aspirate 'h' /h/ as this will tend to blow the vocal folds apart.

1. Begin by making glottal onsets in your speech range.
2. Check that you are retracted and that your effort levels are comfortable. Breath pressure needs to be available and sufficient to the task.
3. Play with pitch, allowing your larynx to rise as you move up in pitch, but staying within your speech quality range. Remember that the higher you go the funnier it needs to be.
4. Begin to energise the glottal onsets, stabilising your larynx from the back and the side with vocal tract anchoring. Stabilise your breath with torso anchoring.
5. Work some sounds starting with a 'y' glide instead of a glottal onset. This helps to keep the tongue in a high position. Some people prefer this onset when moving into belting.
6. Raise your voice to call out on 'Yeah' and 'Yes', or 'Eh' and 'Oy'. Do this on high pitches. Think of being in a noisy street or a crowded bar, when needing to attract someone's attention. Use twang mixed with your energised speech quality to boost your sound levels.
7. Sing an appropriate line from a song that requires this level of energy. Use anything that triggers an auditory memory of loud singing, such as a music hall or vaudeville song, a rock or gospel song, or an archetypical belt song such as *'There's No Business Like Show Business'*. It is absolutely fine to use imitation at this stage; it can help you find your set-up.

You are now close to belting, though you are probably still working in your speech range. In order to access your belt voice you need to 'go up a gear', raising the pitch to *above* where you would normally flip into falsetto, but now increasing the effort levels in retraction and adjusting your head and neck posture so that you are 'looking up to the gods'.

Monitoring the head and neck:
i. Put your hand on top of your head, using the head pat from Chapter 7 (page 77) to elongate and straighten the cervical spine.
ii. Using both hands, monitor the neck for work in the muscles just underneath the occipital bone.
iii. Stabilise the vocal tract from the sides by contracting the 'SCMs' as

described in Exercise 1, Chapter 7 (page 77) 'external anchoring'. In belting you need a strongly lateral sensation in the neck.

iv. Staying in the anchored head position, nod gently up and down, keeping some effort in the back of the neck and at the sides.

v. Notice that, as you nod up, your chin is slightly raised. Avoid pushing the chin forward, which will result in collapsing the back of the neck.

vi. Keep the back of the neck working (it may feel braced or held in this position), and raise the chin a little. Picture yourself in a theatre space, looking up to the highest seats in the auditorium. This is the posture for belting. The sensation is of 'up and back'.

vii. In order to hold this braced position you need support from the body further down. Check that you are working your 'lats' by using the torso anchoring devices from Exercise 3, Chapter 7 (page 81).

Practise doing this without sound. You need to be able to move into this posture easily when getting ready to belt.

Monitoring laryngeal position:

i. Put your fingers on your larynx, feeling for both the thyroid and cricoid cartilages (see Chapter 3, page 20).

ii. Swallow. Notice that your larynx goes up in the first part of the swallow.

iii. Now raise your larynx voluntarily by imitating the squeak of a guinea pig or a mouse. The auditory cue for this is 'EEK!'. This is not the same as whimpering. When you make this sound your larynx usually moves up very quickly, and it may feel as though it has moved away from your finger. If you initiate the tone with a tiny glottal onset you are likely to find the 'tilted cricoid' posture.

iv. Everything feels very small when you do this.

v. Avoid taking a breath to make this noise: you are only raising your larynx and closing your vocal folds. You do not need a lot of air.

vi. Do the squeak again, this time taking a small upper chest breath, holding it for one second before onsetting the sound. This is where your larynx needs to be before you start to belt.

Practise doing this without the anchoring. Just concentrate on moving the larynx into a different position. You are now ready to move on.

8. Repeat stages 1 to 5.

9. Yell or call out on 'Eh' or 'Yeh' as before, starting to hold the end of the word.

10. Continue calling or yelling and sustaining pitch at the end of the word. Keep the same pitch that you used for the call or yell.

11. Sing a phrase that is reminiscent of belting, such as, 'It's gotta happen, happen sometime' from *Cabaret*, or 'I'm in love with a wonderful guy' from *South Pacific* (women), and 'I'm gonna get it, I'm gonna get it soon' from *The Life* (men).

Having found the correct set-up for belting, many clients will comment on how 'easy' it feels. All good voice production is about balanced muscle use, and belting is no exception. If you are singing on an emotional impulse that leads you to belt and you are doing it right, it will feel easy and natural.

Range for belting

Remember that belting is the vocal expression of 'in extremis'. Belting is used above the speech quality range and is there for you to 'top' previous emotional levels. Generally you will only belt one or two notes in a song. Gospel singers can be heard belting up to high A (women) and D a 9th above middle C (men). Women's voices in musical theatre need to be able to belt C, D and E (over an octave above middle C) depending on your type of voice. Men need to be able to belt up to G above middle C (baritones) and between high B and C (tenors). I often find that men's voices can go higher in belt mode than they might otherwise. Used judiciously, belting is perfectly healthy for the voice. It need not 'ruin your head register'; it is simply another way of using your voice. Experienced singers can learn to do both, and I have many clients who can produce excellent 'legit' and belt sounds.

Risks in belting

1. Do not attempt belting until you have mastered speech quality above the gear change. Both speech and twang qualities need to be mastered first.
2. Pay attention to your energy levels when required to belt in a run of performances or during technical week. Remember that when you are tired, it is easy to forget to use your physical support.
3. Women are advised to avoid belting in the pre-menstrual phase of the menstrual cycle. This is because the vocal folds tend to be oedemic (slightly swollen) at this time. During these times, if you cannot rely on your belt, switch to twang or speech with twang. You will probably need to scale down the volume levels at other points in the song so that the song does not lose its dramatic high points.
4. Everyone needs to avoid belting when his or her voice is under par for any reason. Belting is a high-energy voice quality, requiring you to be in good physical and vocal form.

Repertoire for practising belt

Find a song that requires only one or two notes in belt. This is particularly important if you are unfamiliar with belting. Here are some song suggestions:

- Mezzo soprano: '*I'm in Love with a Wonderful Guy*' from *South Pacific*. Work the final sequence of the song.
- Mezzo soprano: '*Don Juan*' from *Smokey Joe's Café*; work the refrain.
- Mezzo soprano: '*Holding to the Ground*' from *Falsettoland* working the section from 'Holding to the ground...' to 'Yes, that's my life...'
- Soprano: '*Your Daddy's Son*' from *Ragtime*. Work the section beginning '...only darkness and pain' to 'I buried my heart in the ground'.
- Soprano: '*I Think I May Want to Remember Today*' from *Starting Here, Starting Now*. Work the sequence building up to 'Albert'.
- Soprano: '*One Night Only*' from *Dream Girls*. Work the section beginning 'I've got one night only'.
- Tenor: '*Bui-Doi*' from *Miss Saigon*, working both of the sections beginning '...they're called Bui-Doi'.
- Tenor: '*Being Alive*' from *Company*, working the final sequence that builds to the end.
- High baritone or tenor: '*What am I Doing?*' from *Closer Than Ever*. Work the last two pages.
- Baritone: '*Make them Hear You*' from *Ragtime*. Work the final fifteen bars.
- Bass: '*I Don't Remember Christmas*' from *Starting Here, Starting Now*. Work from the final build-up to the end.

Mix belting

I am not sure that there is such a thing as a mixed belt, since belting is already a mixed voice quality. There are certainly modifications to the set-up described above. Perhaps this is what people mean by mixed belt. Here is a process that leads to what I have called the 'howl belt'. It produces a more rounded belt voice quality that is suitable for the expression of sorrow, loss and intense longing.

The auditory cue for this type of belting is the sound of loud lamentation 'Oh' or 'Ah', or an extended 'No-'.

Exercise 6: STEPS TO THE 'HOWL BELT'

1. Begin by moaning on pitches in your speech range. Usually we use thin folds in moaning, but you can do it with thick folds if you have practised advancing speech quality.

2. As in stages 1–3 from 'Steps to belting' (page 169) play with pitch, allowing your larynx to rise for the higher pitches.
3. There is some thyroid tilt in this set-up, but you can still use a glottal onset. Work to make more energised glottal onset 'attacks' as your moan turns into a loud lamenting. (If you prefer, use the 'No' cue as an alternative to the glottal onset.)
4. Add twang to boost volume levels.
5. Raise the larynx by making a small squeak, as before.
6. Be sure to anchor the vocal tract at the sides and to engage the torso anchoring muscles.
7. Look 'up to the gods' as before, making sure that the neck feels braced.
8. Sing out on this sound of loud lamentation or howling, using the vowels 'AH' /ɑː/, 'AW' /ɔː/ and 'oh' /əʊ/.

Some clients report more engagement in the abdominal wall in this type of belting. It may be that the breathing is slightly lower than in classic Broadway belting, with more activity in the waistband area.

Song assignment: ALL VOICE QUALITIES

Do this with a partner or group of friends. It's an exercise in imagination, in listening and in vocal control.
1. You take it in turns to sing the same song or group of songs. You should be confident with the notes and the words, preferably off the page.
2. After hearing the song through, your partner asks you to start it again using a specific voice quality.
3. At a suitable point in the song, your partner asks you to change voice quality. You are asked to change again at another suitable point, and continue this process, until you reach the end of the song.
4. Discuss the effect that the changes in voice quality had, and whether or not they represent stylistic and character choices that you feel are appropriate for the song.

You can also try out the following:
5. Your partner asks you to sing a song in different styles, portraying different characters, changing age, status and personal history, and with different dramatic intentions.
6. Your partner identifies which voice qualities you are using in order to effect the changes, while you use your imagination and instinct as an actor to help you in your choices of voice quality.

Commercial voice qualities

In this context 'commercial' refers to musicals that are based around pre-existing popular music. Such musicals would include: *Buddy, Smokey Joe's Café* (rock and roll), *Saturday Night Fever* (the Bee Gees), *Mamma Mia* (Abba), *We Will Rock You* (Queen) and *Tonight's the Night* (Rod Stewart). Sound qualities that go with each of these artists or groups will have their own distinctive features. By using your knowledge of voice qualities, you will probably be able to work out a credible 'mix' that will enable you to be viable for roles in this type of musical. It is impossible to generalise about, or even define, 'pop'. However, high larynx, speech, breathy speech and twang certainly seem to be common features, with belting being used for heavy rock numbers. Shifts of voice quality are rapid in pop music, with changes often being made mid-note and phrase. Here the voice is being used very much as an instrument, and the text is often less important. Vowels will often be general Southern American.

Abusive voice qualities

There is no doubt that some voice qualities used eight times a week may prove to be abusive. These are usually qualities that involve rasp, vocal fold or false fold constriction and the pushing of air into the sound. We are hearing these qualities more and more in cartoon musicals, usually in the comedy and 'baddie' roles. Be aware that some modification is necessary if you are doing a staged version of such a show. There are ways of introducing distortion into your sound without causing vocal trauma, but it needs to be done with technique and used with discrimination. Seek the advice of a good vocal teacher if you are preparing for a role that requires this type of sound quality. A good technician will be able to offer advice and strategies so that you do not endanger your voice during rehearsal or a long run of performances.

Over many years in numerous workshops and one-to-one sessions I have continued to be excited by work on voice quality. I hope that this work will prove as exciting for you too. Working on voice quality not only opens your voice, it enhances your listening skills. Perhaps most importantly for an actor, it enables you access to a wider range of vocal expression that is reliable and repeatable.

Chapter 13
The act of singing

insert Phil Bulcock reference

When you are preparing the text of your song, you are considering both the words and the music. Decisions you ultimately make about your performance will be a balance between these two. The work in this chapter examines what is involved in making these choices and uses work from previous chapters to put them into action. Suggested exercises on text and subtext assume that you have had some dramatic training and allow for you to do character research as you would for a play. In addition, there are considerations such as musical style, the physicality of the character and the dramatic 'play' of the song. Suggested further reading covering these topics in depth are *Successful Singing Auditions*[1] and *On Singing on Stage*.[2]

similar to prepare for any musical character & how you would

Here is a five-point process for preparing dramatic sung text.

1. Consider the meaning, text and context. These will give you a song journey.

2. Consider the musical style and structure.

3. Prepare a phonetic transcription of your song to aid you in working the text.

4. Explore options for vocal characterisation.

5. Prepare a 'song map', indicating changes of thought and choices of voice quality.

We shall now look at Sondheim's '*Anyone Can Whistle*', exploring this process in detail. Use it when preparing new song material.

MEANING TEXT AND CONTEXT

Meaning: the song journey

Prepare your text in detail, just as you would a speech. This includes looking at the function of the song within the context of the entire musical. There are many different approaches to text analysis. The '5 W's' is a simple process that can be used by actors from all backgrounds:

[1] Successful Singing Auditions, Kayes G, Fisher J A&C Black, 2002
[2] On Singing on Stage, Craig, D Applause, 1990

based on STAN!

1. WHO? (Who are you? Know your age, your status, gender and so on.)

2. WHY? (Why are you singing the song? What do you want to achieve by the end of it? How is that a useful stepping stone in the larger journey of the play or musical?)

3. WHAT? (What exactly are you saying in the song?)

4. WHERE? (Where are you when you sing? Be as specific as you can.)

5. WHEN? (When does the song occur? What has happened before and after the song?)

If you can answer these questions you will have a good basis for both a character and a song journey. If you are preparing a song from a musical, then you need to know the answers to these questions within the context of the musical play, but you may well choose to use your own story to provide a different or simply more personal answer to the questions. This is particularly useful when you are auditioning, because it enables you to reveal something about yourself to the auditioning panel.

Using the text of Sondheim's '*Anyone Can Whistle*', go through 'the 5 W's', writing down your answers.

Anyone can whistle, that's what they say – Easy.
Anyone can whistle, any old day – Easy.
It's all so simple: relax, let go, let fly.
So someone tell me why can't I?

I can dance a tango, I can read Greek – Easy.
I can slay a dragon any old week – Easy.
What's hard is simple.
What's natural comes hard.
Maybe you could show me how to let go,
Lower my guard, learn to be free,
Maybe if you whistle, whistle for me.

Here are some questions that frequently arise when I look at this text with an actor:

1. Who are 'they'?

2. Who are you talking to?

3. When are you quoting and when are you commenting?

4. When do the words move to the first person? (This is a significant change.)

5. What changes for the singer in the course of the song?

6. What changes for the audience in the course of the song?

7. What is your mood at the beginning? At the end?

8. Is whistling a metaphor for life, for love, or for anything specific that you find difficult?

Musical and word phrasing

In singing, there is sometimes a tug of war between the word and music phrasing. This can happen when the composer has set long notes where you might not expect them, or has apparently joined thoughts in a musical phrase that do not belong together. Sometimes the tug of war is there for a reason, creating an exciting dynamic between the words and music. Your job is to work with this dynamic to make a dramatic whole. Punctuation and stress are important signals to the meaning and subtext of a song. Follow the punctuation as you would in a text reading.

In 'Anyone Can Whistle', the punctuation is quite precise, indicating when you are quoting other people and when you are speaking for yourself. Compare the musical phrasing with the word phrasing, and notice when they are not quite the same. Even if you do not read music very well, you will spot some discrepancies between the way the words are delivered in speech and their musical setting:

1. Look at the musical phrasing of 'Relax, let go, let fly.' It would be easy to sing straight through this. Follow the guideline of 'sing-as-you-would speak', and mark the commas vocally by making a small stop at each comma. You don't need to take a breath; just stop the sound. These spaces between the notes give the audience time to process the meaning of the text.

2. Look at unstressed syllables that are set to long notes, e.g. 'whis<u>tle</u>', 'sim<u>ple</u>', 'ea<u>sy</u>'. You can rebalance the text by decaying vowels to the end of the note, or allotting some of the note value to final consonants.

Now look at the number of ways the composer has set the word 'easy'; I believe this is a conscious choice on the composer's part. Sometimes it falls, following the inflection of the word, and sometimes it rises. In one place it leaps up through an octave. There are as many ways to inflect the word 'easy' as there are to say 'yes' and 'no' depending on your motivation. For example:

   i. 'Easy': I've been doing it all my life!
   ii. 'Easy': it would be if I knew how.
   iii. 'Easy': I really want to impress you.
   iv. 'Easy': surely everyone knows that!

How might you interpret these long notes? You could use decay, maintain a stable dynamic, or choose to increase volume on the notes. Perhaps you will use more than one of these solutions during the course of the song. Let your choice be determined by dramatic rather than vocal considerations.

A -ny-one can whis-tle, that's what they say, Ea-sy. _____

A -ny-one can whis-tle, a -ny old day, Ea-sy. _____ It's

all so sim -ple: Re - lax, let go, let fly. So

some -one tell me why can't I? _____

I can dance a tan -go, I can read Greek, Ea -sy. _____

I can slay a dra -gon a - ny old week, Ea - sy. _____ What's

hard is sim - ple. What's na -tu - ral comes hard.

May-be you could show me how to let go, low-er my guard, learn to be free,

May -be if you whis -tle, whis -tle for me.

Musical style and structure

Written in 1964, '*Anyone Can Whistle*' is the title song from the show of the same name. I won't attempt to give you the synopsis; it's too complicated, and you can easily look it up for yourself. The setting is contemporary, and there is nothing that indicates a particular vocal style. Structurally, there are two verses and a coda (finishing off section), but the song is constructed to give a through-composed feel rather than of two verses. This is an indication of there being an arrival point by the end of the song.

Making a phonetic script

Here we are applying work learned in Chapter 11. This is a song from an American musical, so we are going to work the text in General American. Begin by counting the sound targets in each word. Make a note of any sounds that you find unusual or difficult. An example might be the word 'natural', which some people pronounce colloquially as two syllables. Sondheim has set the word as three syllables, which is phonetically accurate.

Here's a reminder of the other main points from Chapter 11:

1. Beware of running words into each other that do not belong together, which might change the meaning of the text, e.g. 'it's allso simple' (also simple).

2. Sing the vowels that you would speak. Check out any you are unsure of, using the vowel chart on page 43.

3. Practise saying the vowels with the tongue in a more concave position as in medialising. This will prepare you for matching the vowels in singing.

4. Mark the words that you want to stress using a glottal onset, and mark in any places where you need to stop the voice to delineate punctuation and meaning. Use you own signs to do this.

5. Sing the voiced consonants on pitch, paying particular attention to those on high notes.

6. Make room for the voiceless stops by borrowing time from the written note values.

Here are two scores of the song. The first is a phonetic transcription in General American (page 180), and the second is a musical score (pages 182–3) indicating how the vowels and consonants can be fitted into the musical text.

   i. In this text, note that the 't' /t/ in 'let go' and 'let fly' are not aspirated. This is represented by the marking '⌐'. In this context, the way we would speak them would be to run them together. Sondheim has set the text here to short note values, which matches with the natural speech inflection.

Now look at the music score. This score shows in detail how to make the text work in song. Compare it with the original words and melody as set on page 178:

   i. Notice how much more space the singing score takes up from left to right; every consonant and every vowel has been given its own space in the music.

   ii. Read the phonetic text aloud, following the music score from left to right and noticing the amount of space given on the score for consonants and compound vowels.

Anyone Can Whistle

ɛniwʌn kən hwɪsəl
ðæts hwʌtꟸ ðeɪ seɪ iːzi
ɛniwʌn kən hwɪsəl
ɛni oʊłd deɪ iːzi
ɪts ɑːł soʊ sɪmpəl
rɪlæks lɛtꟸ goʊ lɛtꟸ flaɪ
soʊ sʌmwʌn tɛł miː hwaɪ kænt aɪ

aɪ kən dæns ə tæŋgoʊ
aɪ kən riːd griːk iːzi
aɪ kən sleɪ ə drægən
ɛni oʊłd wiːk iːzi
hwʌts hɑɚd ɪz sɪmpəl
hwʌts næʧɚrəł kʌmz hɑɚd
meɪbi juː kəd ʃoʊ miː
haʊ tə lɛtꟸ goʊ
loʊɚ maɪ gɑɚd lɜːn tə biː friː
meɪbi ɪf juː hwɪsəl
hwɪsəl fɔɚ miː

---

iii. Now sing the text in any comfortable key. Work at thinking speed so that you have time to process the information.

iv. Repeat this process as often as you need to.

v. Sing the song at speed and in the written key.

This music text, using the phonetic transcription, is very detailed. Very rarely does a composer indicate such precise intentions to the singer. Indeed, it might be thought to impose an undesirable rigidity on the performer if the composer were to do this. Nevertheless, the decisions about making the sung text intelligible need to be made. Working out how is part of making the song 'your own'.

Vocal characterisation

Which voice quality best conveys to the audience your psychological state at any point in the song? Here are some factors you might like to consider. Remember that these are only the beginning of a process, and that some answers will change during the course of rehearsal.

1. The '5 W's'. Who am I? What do I want? How am I going to get it? What is in my way? Where am I? Why am I here? When is it? What am I doing? What is my action?

2. Internal factors. What are my needs and desires? What is my social background? Ethnic values? Physiology? Psychological peculiarities or ways of thinking of the character?

3. External factors. What are my relationships with, or attitudes towards, other characters? (In some interpretations of a song, this may only involve the person to whom the song is directed.) What is my social environment? Physical environment? Are there any specific immediate circumstances to take into consideration?

Below I have set out two alternative song journeys. Different voice qualities are implied in each reading of the song. Remember that the choice of voice qualities is a subjective one; you may well go for something quite different from the ones I've given, based on your own story and changes of intention. That is absolutely fine: the point of the exercise is to make decisions.

Journey 1

At the beginning of the song you are resentful and cynical. (Ask yourself, 'who are they trying to kid?') In the second section, bravado kicks in. (Tell them you can do this and that.) Then you become more thoughtful and vulnerable, with a big change on the word 'maybe'. But that is too much for you, and you finish the song in cynical mode.

See page 184 for a short score of the music (tune and text only) indicating suggested changes of voice quality for this scenario.

Journey 2

At the beginning of the song you are uncertain and wistful. (You think of what you wish you could do too.) You begin to encourage and cheer yourself. (You think of the things you can do.) You become more positive, hopeful and open. (Life isn't what I expected, but you can see there are people around to help.)

The suggestions for voice qualities are different for this journey (see page 185).

Mapping out your song

When learning new material you need to make a complete map of your song, including changes of thought, dynamic, voice quality, stress and breathing marks. Subtext may also be included. This map represents the choices you have made either alone or in conjunction with other actors,

applies to any role — ADAPTATION, just extends to MD & choreographer too

the musical director and director during the rehearsal process. Two song assignments follow, dealing with decisions about the song journey that might indicate changes of voice quality. The suggested reading for these songs is obviously personal and not intended to be definitive. Work them as an exercise in making choices. If you disagree, know why and make decisions that reflect how *you* would interpret the text.

Song assignment 1: 'WITH EVERY BREATH I TAKE'

Here is a song from Cy Coleman's *City of Angels* (lyrics by David Zippel). In the show it is sung by a woman, but may be sung out of context by a man as the text isn't gender-specific. This song may also be performed as a solo cabaret number, which is how it appears in the show. Here's the text:

A section

**There's not a morning that I open up my eyes
and find I didn't dream of you.
Without a warning, though it's never a surprise,
soon as I awake,
thoughts of you arise
with ev'ry breath I take.**

Bridge section

**At any time or place I close my eyes and see your face
and I'm embracing you.
If only I believed that dreams come true.
Darling,**

A section

**You were the one who said forever from the start and I've been
drifting since you've gone,
out on a lonely sea that only you can chart.
I've been going on
knowing that my heart will break
with every breath I take.**

This song is written in a very traditional ABA form. It would be easy to perform this song as a torch song for an unresolved lost love, but it can be read another way too.

There is, for instance, no need to let the audience know until you sing the word 'if' that all is not well. You could start the song in a state of happy luxuriance, enjoying the feelings that this person evokes in you, until you bring yourself up short in the final section. Cy Coleman has cleverly made the music overlap into this section to fool the audience for a little longer. So, if this is the outline of your scenario, what voice qualities are implied?

Remember that different voice qualities will mean different things in a different setting, and even a 'happy' voice quality can change if it is delivered with sarcasm, so what I'm offering here is will again be subjective. Voice qualities indicating a state of happiness might be:

i. breathy speech (diffuse, sensual, laid back);
ii. speech with cry (warm and deep);
iii.cry (very soft and silky tone).

The tempo is slow, so I don't feel twang is indicated; the feel would be too upbeat. Pay special attention to the last line of the first section 'with ev'ry breath I take', because you are going to repeat it at the end of the song with a totally different emphasis. You might want to make this line extra soft in dynamic, or change quality for it. Within the overall quality you choose for the section, a change of quality might be indicated when you have a sub-clause qualifying what you have just said: 'though it's never a surprise'.

The bridge section needs to build in intensity: the feelings become more pressing, real and immediate. This is reflected in the rising melodic line of the music so you need to go with it:

1. If you started in breathy speech, you might like to move into speech with cry (intensity and warmth).

2. If you started in cry (or mixed it with speech), you might want to move into twang. Remember that you can add twang to any voice quality to increase its intensity.

3. Within this overall change there are words and phrases in which you might want a different quality, e.g. 'and I'm embracing you'.

4. What ever you decide, there must be a change at the word 'if'. Remember that to get suddenly soft and breathy can be just as shocking as changing to a louder voice quality. (Think of people who go quiet when they are angry!)

The last section could be construed as accusatory, sarcastic, bitter:

1. Speech quality can be angry, especially when mixed with twang.

2. Twang on its own could be sarcastic.

3. The short phrases that build to the end ('I've been going on, knowing that my heart will break') need to build to a climax, and belt quality is indicated here. (Men who are not basses will want this song transposed up a little in order to get the belt. The pitch is too low otherwise to make this quality.)

4. After the belt, you must decide how you want to deliver the last line. What effect do you want to have on the audience or person to whom the song is addressed? You could choose:

i. speech quality for resignation;
ii. falsetto quality for regret or a sigh;
iii.speech and twang for anger;
iv. cry quality for a sense of staying with the feeling of painful loss.

Song assignment 2: 'IF THE HEART OF A MAN' (MEN); 'WHEN MY HERO IN COURT APPEARS' (WOMEN)

This assignment can be worked in pairs or in a group. The aim is to sing the songs using the voice qualities indicated. Perform your chosen song unseen, either with your back to the listener, or recording onto a tape or minidisc. What psychological states were conveyed through the voice qualities you used? Did they have the effect you expected? If not, explore or discuss what might be changed in order to create the response you want in the listener. Both songs are from John Gay's *The Beggar's Opera*.

The first song is sung by Macheath, quite early on in the opera, before he is tricked by Polly's parents.

The second song is sung by Polly Peachum as she tries to dissuade her father from going ahead with arraigning her lover.

Will the process of song mapping stop you from being 'in the moment'? I don't think so. Some of the most exciting performances I have heard in workshops with actors have come about when they have been asked to focus on something very specific such as an aspect of the text, phrasing or articulation. Focussing in this way seems to free the part of the actor that knows how to connect with the material and allows something instinctive to come out. I can only suggest you try it.

Afterword

Over the last three years, since the publication of the first edition of *Singing and The Actor*, I have worked the material with numerous performers in workshops and in private sessions. I have also had the privilege of imparting the techniques to other teachers. They in turn have adapted and developed the material to suit their students and teaching environment. Along the way there has been plenty of discussion and feedback. In this way teaching practice is a shared venture, and I am enormously grateful for the insight I have gained as a result of this interaction. Pedagogy cannot remain fixed; it needs to reflect and support the needs of performance practice, rather than the other way around. You, the actor, are in the front line of change, working to express, explore and deliver text with honesty and insight. I very much hope that the work in this book had provided a foundation for just that.

GLOSSARY

Alveolar ridge The ridge of gum behind the upper front teeth.

Arytenoid cartilages Small pyramid shaped structures that sit on the shoulders of the cricoid cartilage. The back of the vocal folds attach to them.

Bel canto Literally meaning 'beautiful singing' and originally referring to a specific school of Italian singing. Now used more loosely to indicate a style of singing where beauty of sound and vocal line are paramount over other performance considerations.

Cervical spine The first seven vertebrae of the spinal column.

Changes of registration The points where the vocal folds change length and thickness, resulting in a change of voice quality.

Compulsory Figures Jo Estill's training system for voice 'Model for Compulsory Figures, Level One', © EVTS 1997.

Connective tissue This exists around the muscles in the body enabling them to move smoothly.

False vocal folds These consist of tissue and fatty matter, and their function is to make a tight seal in the larynx to protect the airways.

Formants The resonance frequencies of the vocal tract.

Frequency The number of cycles per second, hence frequency of vibration of the vocal folds. This factor largely determines the pitch of the voice.

Fricatives These sounds are characterised by a continuous airstream passing through an obstructed vocal tract.

Glottal This means 'of the glottis'.

Glottis This is a notional term, referring to the space between the vocal folds. Hence we close the glottis when we make sound, and open it when we are breathing in.

Glossus Tongue or of the tongue, hence glossal.

Harmonic A component frequency of wave motion.

Hertz The unit of frequency (number of cycles per second).

Isolation checklist A sequence of physical movements devised to help you isolate muscles used in tasks.

Larynx The thyroid and cricoid cartilages, the epiglottis and the hyoid bone. (The larynx is sometimes referred to as the 'voice box'.)

Legit Literally an abbreviation of legitimate. In musical theatre it usually refers to a style of singing that is more classical.

Mandible The jaw bone.

Nasal port The doorway between the nasal and oral cavities (also called the velar-pharyngeal port).

Occipital groove The depression at the base of the skull.

Onset The start of sound; in singing it refers to specifically how we bring the vocal folds together.

Palato-glossus The muscle linking the back of the tongue and soft palate used to lift the back of the tongue upwards for sounds such as 'k'.

Palato pharyngeus A paired muscle of the soft palate that helps to raise the larynx in swallowing.

Passaggio The point of transition between the vocal registers

Pharynx The tube of the vocal tract.

Pilates system A complete approach to developing body awareness and an easy physicality in day-to-day life, recommended by health experts as a safe form of exercise.

Plosive A class of sound characterised by a complete occlusion of the vocal tract; there is a build-up of pressure, followed by release.

Raised plane position This describes the position of the vocal folds in relation to the posterior cricoarytenoid muscles, which can abduct, elevate, and elongate the vocal folds.

Retraction From retract, meaning to withdraw or pull back. Used by Estill to describe the action of the false vocal false in the laugh posture

Simple vowels Single vowel sounds (also called monophthongs); they can be either long or short.

Siren An exercise deriving from Lilli Lehman and developed to work on vocal awareness and range. The sound is made in imitation a police or ambulance siren, hence the name.

Spectrogram A sound spectrogram (or sonogram) is a visual representation of an acoustic signal.

Subglottic pressure The pressure of air beneath the vocal folds.

Supraglottic pressure The pressure of air above the vocal folds.

Supra-hyoid The muscles and structure above the hyoid bone.

Vocalis The muscle of the vocal fold or thyroarytenoid.

Voice Analysis software A good place to start browsing is on the Vocal Software listing at Vocalist. http://www.vocalist.org.uk. Also recommended are VoceVista http://www.vocevista.com/ and Visualization Software LLC http://www.visualizationsoftware.com/

Vibratory cycle The disturbance of air which makes up the sound source.

LIST OF GENERAL EXERCISES, AWARENESS EXERCISES AND SONG ASSIGNMENTS

Chapter 1
Awareness exercise 1: The vibrating mechanism
Awareness exercise 2: Closing the vocal folds
Awareness exercise 3: Locating the soft palate
Awareness exercise 4: The siren

Chapter 2
Awareness exercise 1: Constriction
Awareness exercise 2: Retraction
Awareness exercise 3: Auditory monitoring using silent breathing
Awareness exercise 4: Monitoring personal effort
Awareness exercise 5: The glottal onset
Awareness exercise 6: The aspirate onset
Awareness exercise 7: The simultaneous onset

Chapter 3
Awareness exercise 1: General awareness
Awareness exercise 2: Feeling the larynx
Awareness exercise 3: Raising and lowering your larynx
Awareness exercise 4: Moving the larynx forwards and backwards
Awareness exercise 5: Tilting the thyroid
Awareness exercise 6: Moving from neutral to tilted thyroid
Awareness exercise 7: Tilting the cricoid
Awareness exercise 8: Changing vocal fold plane

Chapter 4
Exercise 1: The elastic recoil
Exercise 2: Working the recoil with rhythm
Awareness exercise 1: The waistband
Awareness exercise 2: The abdominal wall (top and bottom)
Awareness exercise 3: The diamond
Exercise 3: Working to sustain
Awareness exercise 4: Reviewing onset of tone
Awareness exercise 5: Consonants
Song assignment: Your song

Chapter 5
Exercise 1: The three positions of the false vocal folds
Exercise 2: External monitoring

Exercise 3: Random sirening
Exercise 4: Targeting your breaks
Exercise 5: Octave sirens
Exercise 6: From siren to vowel
Song assignment: Your song

Chapter 6
Awareness exercise 1: Finding the seal
Awareness exercise 2: Moving the soft palate
Awareness exercise 3: What moves where?
Exercise 1: Opening and closing
Exercise 2: Opening and closing with all vowels
Exercise 3: Half-open nasal port
Exercise 4: Half-open to closed nasal port
Exercise 5: Opening and closing the nasal port while singing scales
Exercise 6: Palato pharyngeus and the 'lift'
Exercise 7: Making a decrescendo with the soft palate
Song assignment 1: Mirening
Song assignment 2: Your song
Song assignment 3: Happy Birthday
Song assignment 4: Amazing Grace

Chapter 7
Awareness exercise 1: Thick folds
Awareness exercise 2: Thin folds
Awareness exercise 3: Raised vocal fold plane
Exercise 1: External anchoring
Exercise 2: Internal anchoring
Exercise 3: Anchoring the torso
Exercise 4: Messa di voce or dynamic control
Exercise 5: Working the range
Exercise 6: Thinning the vocal folds to ascend the scale
Exercise 7: Raising the larynx to ascend to scale
Exercise 8: Thickening the folds to descend the scale
Exercise 9: Lowering the larynx to descend the scale
Song assignment: The Balcony Scene (Tonight) – Tony and Maria (West Side Story)

Chapter 8
Awareness exercise 1: How the jaw works
Awareness exercise 2: Giving in to gravity with the jaw
Awareness exercise 3: The hanging jaw position
Awareness exercise 4: Monitoring jaw movement

Awareness exercise 5: The tongue
Exercise 1: The tongue back
Exercise 2: Separating the action of the tongue and soft palate
Exercise 3: Medialising – stage 1
Exercise 4: Medialising – stage 2
Song assignment 1: Anyone Can Whistle; Your song
Exercise 5: Working the lips
Exercise 6: Lengthening the vocal tract with the lips
Song assignment 2: Your song

Chapter 9
Exercise 1: Preparation for twang
Exercise 2: Tightening the twanger
Exercise 3: Twanging
Exercise 4: Twanging with all vowels
Exercise 5: Twanging through the range
Exercise 6: Oral twang
Exercise 7: Nasal to oral twang

Chapter 10
Song assignment 1: Your song
Song assignment 2: Targeting gear changes
Song assignment 3: Managing sudden leaps in the range with 'Anyone Can Whistle'
Song assignment 4: Targeting insufficient airflow and locking with 'I've Never Been In Love Before'
Song assignment 5: Targeting breathy tone with 'I've Never Been In Love Before'
Song assignment 6: Targeting over-breathing with 'I've Never Been In Love Before'
Song assignment 7: Targeting lack of sustaining power with 'I've Never Been In Love Before'
Song assignment 8: Targeting excessive vibrato with your song
Song assignment 9: Adding the voice-body connection with 'If I Loved You'
Song assignment 10: Changing vocal fold mass with 'If I Loved You'
Song assignment 11: Projection via the singer's formant with your song
Song assignment 12: The opening phrase of 'With Every Breath I Take' by Cy Coleman and David Zippel
Song assignment 13: The bridge passage of 'Empty Chairs At Empty Tables' by Schönberg and Boubil
Song assignment 14: 'Autumn' From Starting Here, Starting Now by Maltby and Shire (1)

Song assignment 15: 'Autumn' From Starting Here, Starting Now by Maltby and Shire (2)

Chapter 11
Exercise 1: Pitching and muscularity
Exercise 2: Releasing voiced consonants
Awareness exercise: An up-tempo patter song

Chapter 12
Awareness exercise: Exploring your vocal set-up
Exercise 1: Steps to speech quality
Exercise 2: Steps to falsetto quality
Exercise 3: Steps to cry quality
Exercise 4: Steps to twang quality
Exercise 5: Steps to belting
Exercise 6: Steps to the 'howl belt'
Song assignment: All voice qualities

Chapter 13
Song assignment 1: 'With Every Breath I Take'
Song assignment 2: 'If The Heart Of A Man' (men); 'When My Hero In Court Appears' (women)

INDEX

INDEX OF SONG TITLES